R.L. Stine

Dear Readers:

I had so much fun with this book, it's FRIGHTENING!

I hope you enjoy my life as much as I have!

SCARY Best Wishes,

RL Stine

IT CAME FROM OHIO!
MY LIFE AS A WRITER

IT CAME FROM OHIO!
MY LIFE AS A WRITER

by R.L. Stine
As told to Joe Arthur

SCHOLASTIC INC.
New York   Toronto   London   Auckland   Sydney

A PARACHUTE PRESS BOOK

ISBN 0-590-36674-2
Copyright © 1997 by Parachute Press, Inc.
All rights reserved. Published by Scholastic Inc.

12 11 10 9 8 7 6 5 4 3 2 1   7 8 9/9 0 1 2/0

Printed in the U.S.A.
First Scholastic printing, April 1997

• CONTENTS •

• INTRODUCTION •

by Joe Arthur

.L. Stine was not America's best-selling author when I met him. And he wasn't called R.L. Stine.

"The name is Stine," he said. "Bob Stine."

The meeting took place when we were college students at Ohio State University. I can still see him, typing at a desk in the back of the *Sundial* office.

Sundial was the campus humor magazine. Written and edited by students, *Sundial*'s cartoons, comics, jokes, and articles all made fun of college life.

Bob's official title at *Sundial* that year was "Contributor." Contributors turned in stories and jokes to the magazine.

I came to the office because I had written an

incredibly funny spoof about a space flight. I could hardly wait to give it to the editor.

The editor had other things on his mind. He was in a panic. He said the printing company had moved up the deadline to three o'clock that afternoon.

"Bob, are you going to have that story finished?" the editor wanted to know. The editor was so nervous he had chewed his fingernails completely off. I thought any moment he was going to start on his toes.

Bob just nodded and kept on typing.

I thought the editor was kidding me when he said Bob was writing the *whole* magazine. Turned out he wasn't kidding. This was nothing new to Bob. He had been writing and editing his own magazines since he was in fourth grade. And it was very funny stuff. That's important in humor magazines.

With time running out, Bob really hammered away on that typewriter. Except maybe "hammer" isn't the right word.

Not too many people know this—but R.L. Stine is a one-finger typist! That's not to say he has only one finger. He has five of them on each hand. What I mean is, R.L. Stine types his stories with one finger.

Luckily for me that day at the *Sundial* office, Bob suddenly grabbed that one finger. He was hurt! In a frantic last-minute rush to finish the issue, Bob had jammed his finger between two keys. The typewriter was fine, but Bob had a serious injury. His typing finger was scratched!

• IT CAME FROM OHIO! •

It was lucky for me only because there was now space in the magazine for *my* piece. And so, on that same day in 1962, an article of mine was printed—*and* I met R.L. Stine. He has been my best friend ever since.

Bob never forgets my birthday, and I never forget to remind him of his. When Bob was writing funny books and magazines, his choice in birthday gifts ran mostly to rubber chickens. Now that he's the king of scary stories, R.L. is beyond rubber chickens. The past five birthdays he hasn't sent me a single one. Now he sends me rubber *eyeballs*.

I've followed Bob's writing career from his years as editor of *Sundial*, through his jobs with fan magazines, trade magazines, and funny books. I've been with Bob when he was just another face in the crowd. And I've seen the traffic-stopping celebrity who is swamped by thousands of fans wanting his autograph.

He sure stopped traffic when he came back to his hometown of Columbus, Ohio, for a book signing.

You should have seen the mob of people and cars trying to get into the bookstore parking lot! Streets were tied up in all four directions. The store manager told us he had never seen such a large crowd to meet an author. "It was amazing," he said.

R.L. Stine's life as a writer is pretty amazing. And it is a pretty good story. It's the story of how my friend—a young man with a portable typewriter and a lot of crazy ideas—went from making up little magazines at home in his room to becoming the best-selling American author of all time.

More than three million copies of Bob's *Goosebumps* and *Fear Street* are snapped up every month. There is hardly a kid in America under the age of fifteen who is not familiar with the works of R.L. Stine. Such a huge following means Bob has typed his way into history.

And he's done it all with one finger!

But I've gone on long enough. All the rest of this story is in Bob's words. I have written it down just as he told it to me. Enjoy....

Joe Arthur

IT CAME FROM OHIO!

MY LIFE AS A WRITER

"I made my most important discovery when I was seven...."

I was born October 8, 1943, in Columbus, Ohio. My parents called me Robert Lawrence Stine (now you know what the R.L. stands for). One of my earliest memories is a scary one. It's about Whitey.

Whitey was our dog. In pictures, Whitey looks like he was half husky, half collie, and half elephant. He was so big that when we allowed him in the house, he knocked over vases—and the tables they were on! That's why we kept him in the garage.

When I was four, it was my job to let Whitey out of the garage every morning. As soon as I stepped outside, I could hear him scratching at the inside of the garage door.

Slowly, I'd push up the heavy door. And Whitey would come charging out at me. His tail would wag furiously and he would bark like crazy. He was so glad to see me!

Barking and crying, he would leap on me—and knock me to the driveway. Every morning!

"Down, Whitey! Down!" I begged.

THUD! I was down on the driveway.

THUD! Every morning.

Whitey was a good dog. But I think he helped give me my scary view of life. I wonder if I would have become a horror writer if I didn't start every morning when I was four flat on my back on the driveway!

I grew up in the town of Bexley. Bexley is a suburb of Columbus, and Columbus is right in the middle of Ohio.

When I was little, we lived in a three-story house. We had a big yard with a lot of shade trees.

My brother, Bill, is three years younger than me. He and I shared a bedroom on the second floor. The third floor was an attic. It was strictly forbidden. Mom told us never to go up there.

I asked her why. She only shook her head and said, "Don't ask."

That attic from my childhood is also one of the reasons why I write *Goosebumps* and *Fear Street* today.

I used to lie in my bed at night and stare at the ceiling. *What terrible thing is up there in the attic?*

"Two weeks old, with my mom.
I'm the one wearing the dress."

"Look at me. One year old
and way more hair than I have now!"

I wondered. I pretended I could see through the plaster. Of course I couldn't see anything. Except plaster. But my imagination sure could.

In my imagination, a coatrack stood at the top of the attic stairs. Next to it a three-legged table, several cardboard cartons, and an old windup record player. That dark shape back in the corner was a mysterious, old trunk. Oh, and there was a dusty moosehead. I could see this stuff as clear as day. But it was only furniture. It wasn't scary.

The scary part was the monster in the attic. I made it up. And I made up stories about the monster with trunks and mooseheads. These stories seem silly to me now, but at the time they were the best answer I could come up with to the question, *What's in the attic?*

I knew it had to be something truly awful. Otherwise my mom wouldn't make such a big deal about it.

So I didn't go up to the attic. Not right away.

This doesn't mean I had a weird, haunted childhood. I didn't.

My family was a typical family. Dad worked for a restaurant supply company, and Mom was a housewife. We didn't have much money. But my parents worked hard to make sure we never felt poor. There were three of us kids—me, Bill, and my sister, Pam, who came along when I was seven.

My favorite activity as a kid?

Listening to the radio. Believe it or not, we didn't get a TV until I was nine. So I spent hours and hours listening to the radio.

When I was a kid, radio wasn't just music and talk shows. There were wonderful stories, mysteries, comedies, and westerns on the radio every night. I would listen to such exciting shows as *The Lone*

"My first house had a big yard
with a built-in barbecue, a fish pond,
and a bird bath."

• IT CAME FROM OHIO! •

Ranger, *The Shadow*, *The Whistler*, and *Gang Busters*. There was one show that *terrified* me. It was called *Suspense*. I still remember how scary it was. In the beginning of the show, a long gong would chime. And then a very creepy announcer with a deep voice would say: "And now... tales... calculated... to keep you in... SUSPENSE!" His voice was so terrifying, it gave me chills. And I'd reach out and click off the radio before the scary story would come on.

I never heard one story. I was too scared.

I still remember that creepy voice. Today, I try to make my books as scary as that announcer's voice on the *Suspense* radio show.

I had a big, powerful radio that could pull in radio stations from all over. As I became older, my favorite stations were in New York City.

One New York station had a man named Jean Shepherd on the air every night. Shepherd is a wonderful storyteller. He's the guy who wrote the movie *A Christmas Story*. I like the scene where the kid gets his tongue frozen to a flagpole. If you see the movie, that's Jean Shepherd narrating it too.

Shepherd's radio show was broadcast live, from midnight to early morning. Shepherd told wonderful, funny stories about his childhood, about his family and friends, and about New York City.

I loved the guy's humor. I loved the way he made up stories. And I started dreaming about someday going

7

to New York. I think everyone dreams of faraway places. I know I did. I couldn't imagine living anywhere but New York City. I still can't.

If Jean Shepherd awakened in me a love of storytelling and New York, he awakened my parents too! Mainly because I was up late on school nights laughing like an idiot! My parents could stand it only so long. Finally, Mom would scream upstairs, "Turn off that radio!"

I never did.

Late at night, when we were supposed to be asleep, Bill and I gave each other goosebumps.

We would lie in our beds, stare up at the shifting shadows on the ceiling, and take turns telling each other scary stories.

Our stories were about ghosts and haunted houses, werewolves and mummies. Some were about walking through the woods near our house. Monsters leaped out from behind trees. Werewolves howled and bats fluttered.

My usual plot in those days had a little kid—a kid who looked and sounded very much like my brother—being chased around his house by one of my monsters....

The kid is in his room, and he's terrified.

All he got was a glimpse of the thing. What is it? The boy doesn't know. It looked like a man, like a big, stooped man. But the head—it wasn't exactly a man's head. Men didn't have faces with fins and dripping lizard scales.

8

• IT CAME FROM OHIO! •

The kid can hear the footsteps. The thing is searching the other bedrooms. Where should the boy hide? He hasn't got much time. Should he hide in the closet? What about under the bed?

No way! The monster would look in those places first.

The kid starts running. Forget about making noise! Hurry! Out in the hall. The kid reaches the landing. He scrambles down the stairs. Two, three steps at a time.

Don't trip! he tells himself, screams to himself.

The lizard-monster is right behind him. It's so close, the boy can hear it hiss, feel its hot breath on the back of his neck.

And he can see that he'll never reach the front door alive. The door is too far away.

The kid makes for the hall closet instead. He yanks open the door.

The kid stops. His eyes open wide. He is shocked by what he sees in the closet. Stunned! It's horrible. Gruesome. The kid starts to scream.

At that moment in the story I would stop. "Turn out the light, Bill," I would say. "Time to go to sleep."

"Huh?" This made Bill very upset. "That's not fair!" he would cry. "What's in the closet? What about the monster? Does he get the kid? Come on, tell me! Finish the story, Bob!"

"Sorry. Too tired," I would reply, yawning. "Good night. I'll finish the story tomorrow."

And I would fall asleep with a cruel smile on my face, leaving my brother in total suspense.

Today, in my scary books, I do the same trick at the end of every chapter. I try to leave my readers in the same state of shock and suspense that I left my brother in, all those years ago.

These stories Bill and I shared in our house in Ohio were a clue to our futures. We both turned out to be writers. And the creatures from the dark woods, the frightening shadows that came alive in our walls, the mummies and the werewolves—they all followed me into my *Goosebumps* and *Fear Street* books.

Why did I like scary stories when I was a kid?

I think because I found the *real* world pretty scary. I was a fearful kid. I wasn't bold or adventurous. I liked staying in my room and writing stories and making little magazines and comics.

When my parents sent me to day camp one summer, I wasn't very happy about it. At day camp, I had one of my scariest, most panic-stricken, embarrassing moments. It happened at the end of camp.

All campers had to demonstrate our swimming skills to get our Red Cross badges. I was in the beginner Tadpole group. I had my Tadpole badge. I was trying for the next badge—the Turtle.

To get a Turtle badge, swimmers had to jump into the pool, swim to the other side, then swim back. We

"That's Bill on the left and me on the right.
This time, my sister, Pam, is wearing the dress."

Tadpoles all lined up at the edge of the pool. We would take turns jumping in, one by one.

As I got closer and closer to the front of the line, panic swept over me. I knew I couldn't jump in. I could swim easily from one end of the pool to the other. But the idea of *jumping* into the pool froze me in terror. What was I going to do?

The whole camp was watching. All the counselors. All the kids.

My turn.

I stepped up to the edge of the pool.

I gazed into the water.

I froze. I knew I couldn't do it. I couldn't jump in. Everyone was calling to me, urging me to jump, calling out support.

"JUMP!" they called. "YOU CAN DO IT! JUMP!"

But I couldn't move. I couldn't breathe. I was too afraid.

I turned and walked away.

It was a moment of total panic. And I think back to that moment whenever I write about a kid who is really terrified. I remember how I felt—and I try to write that same feeling of fear into my character.

To this day, I have to *climb* into a swimming pool. I can't jump in.

My eight-year-old nephews think it's very funny. They're always teasing me and trying to get me to jump. They think it's funny that a horror writer is afraid to jump into a swimming pool.

Maybe they're right. But I also guess it's important for a horror writer to know *true* horror!

One day, when I was about seven years old, I saw a FOR SALE sign in my front yard.

I asked my mother what was going on. She shrugged and told me, "We have to move." I didn't understand such things then, but I learned later that

"Here I am at day camp.
I'm the one standing on the far left.
The kid sitting in front of me is my
close friend, Norm."

Dad had changed jobs. We couldn't afford such a big house anymore.

I decided if I wanted to discover the secret of the attic, it had to be now. That night I told Bill about my plan.

"When Mom finds out," Bill said, "you're going to get it."

"If you say anything," I warned him, "Captain Grashus will get you!"

That shut him up. He was scared to death of Captain Grashus.

And who was Captain Grashus?

Captain Grashus was the world's strongest, bravest, most invincible superhero. I know because I made him up.

In fact, *I* was Captain Grashus.

Dressed in his super suit—a bath towel tied around the neck like a cape—the Captain could outmuscle Superman and declaw Catwoman, all with one hand tied behind his back.

In my dreams.

Mostly the Captain ruled our bedroom.

Bill was the Grashus *Ranger*. The Ranger's job was to do exactly what Captain Grashus told him. No questions asked. It was great to be the older brother!

Sometimes Captain Grashus's orders included non-superhero-type activities, like mowing the grass or cleaning our room. It's hard to believe, but Bill didn't always want to play the Grashus Ranger game.

And this was one of those times. Even Captain Grashus couldn't make Bill go up in the attic.

I wasn't in the mood to argue. What I was in the mood to do was go upstairs. I had to see for myself the secret in the attic.

SCHOOL DAYS
1951 – 52

"Me, age eight—scary!"

I eased open the door. The attic steps led up into an inky blackness. I didn't have a flashlight.

Captain Grashus wouldn't let a little darkness stop him. The only trouble was, there was a *lot* of darkness.

So the Captain snapped on the light. The switch sounded like a cannon.

Had Mom and Dad heard? No. Not a creature was stirring, not even my parents.

Slowly, one step at a time, I started up into the attic.

Something touched my face! What was it? Was it the attic monster?

No. A cobweb.

I continued to climb. The attic floor was dusty and uneven. I looked around. It was a total disappointment. No trunks. No moosehead.

What a letdown!

The only thing in the entire place seemed to be a clothes rack. Mom's out-of-style dresses and some of Dad's old workpants. I started to turn around when I noticed a small black case on the floor.

I walked over and picked up the case. It was coated with dust. The handle squeaked.

I carried the case over to the stairs and sat down. There was a lock on the case.

I snapped it open.

I stared into that small black case. But I had no idea what an important discovery I had just made.

· 2 ·

"You think you're pretty funny, don't you?"

"What is it?" I heard Bill whisper. He was standing at the bottom of the attic stairs peering up. "What did you find up there?"

"It's a portable typewriter," I told him. I struck a couple keys with my index finger. "And it works."

I was so excited about finding the typewriter! I started down the attic stairs. But the figure looming in the doorway below made me hesitate. It wasn't my brother. And it certainly wasn't a cobweb.

It was my mother. Her arms were folded and she was frowning.

"I warned you about the attic," she said. "The floors are rotting. It isn't safe."

What could I say? I was caught.

My mother sent me to my room.

The good news is she let me keep the typewriter. I started typing immediately. With one finger.

I suppose later, when I got to high school, I should have taken a typing class and learned to type with more than one finger. But it was too late. I was already typing at lightning speed with just one finger. So I stuck with it.

I might have developed the fastest finger in the Midwest. But at seven years of age I wasn't quite ready to write books. I didn't start my first book until I was twelve.

In the beginning, I wanted to draw comics.

For as long as I can remember I've loved comic books. I wanted in the worst way to draw some myself. And that's how I did draw them—*in the worst way!* It took me a long time to accept the fact that I cannot draw at all. But I didn't let it stop me.

From the moment I found that typewriter, I began writing and illustrating my own magazines and comics.

I wanted to draw comics like EC comics. EC was a small company that put out horror and science fiction comics. And *Mad. Mad* was an EC comic before it became a full-size magazine. I thought *Mad* was hilarious, and I inhaled the grossness of EC's *Tales from the Crypt* and *Vault of Horror.* I loved them.

My mother had a different opinion. She said these comics were trash. She wouldn't let me bring them in the house. I was an unhappy kid until I realized they had *Mad* and all my other favorites at the barber shop.

"I thought you just got a haircut," my mother said every Saturday morning when I asked her for a dollar to pay the barber.

I spent just about every Saturday reading in the barber shop. Not until I'd read all the way to the inside back cover did I finally climb into the chair for my usual ten-second trim. I spent so much time at the barber shop that the barber started calling me "son."

When I wasn't getting my hair cut, I became a one-person magazine factory.

I think *The All New Bob Stine Giggle Book* was my first magazine. I still have one copy of this masterpiece. Typed on the old typewriter, it is three by four inches, tiny compared to newsstand magazines.

The Giggle Book is ten pages thick, but has only five pages of text. For some reason, I didn't type on both sides of the paper. This miniature magazine is filled with jokes and riddles. The best joke in the issue, I think, is this one:

Ted: I saw you pushing your bicycle to work.

Ned: I was so late I didn't have time to get on it.

HAH, For Maniacs Only!! came out in 1956. The blurb on the cover promised, "All in this issue, Howdy Deedy, The 64-Thousand-Dollar Answer and Dragnut." Like *Mad*, I was spoofing popular TV shows. (*Howdy Doody* was a popular kids' show. *The $64,000 Question* was a quiz show, and *Dragnet* was a police show.) I drew the pictures myself.

I spent hours and hours on these little magazines. My tools included the typewriter, pens, pencils, crayons, tape, paste, and scissors. The stapler was probably the highest-tech piece of equipment I had.

We didn't have personal computers when I was a kid. I would have gone completely *bananas* with a Power Mac and one of those desktop publishing programs!

It was a big job, making one copy of each issue. And that's all I made—one copy. After showing off my creation to Bill, I took the latest issue to school and passed it around for my friends to read.

I tried to poke fun at everyone in my magazines. People in general and no one in particular. Harvey Poobah, for instance, was a character I made up. In *FEEF* magazine, "Harvey Poobah fell off the Empire State Building and lived. (Until he hit the ground.)"

In another issue, I warned my readers that "more accidents occur on the basement steps than in any other place in the house. Play it safe! When you go down to the basement, don't use the steps!"

I experimented with titles. *Ming* was one of the more unusual. I also used *Tales to Drive You Batty*, *Whammy*, and *Stine's Line*. One of my favorites was *BARF*. *BARF* consisted of funny captions placed under pictures I cut out of magazines.

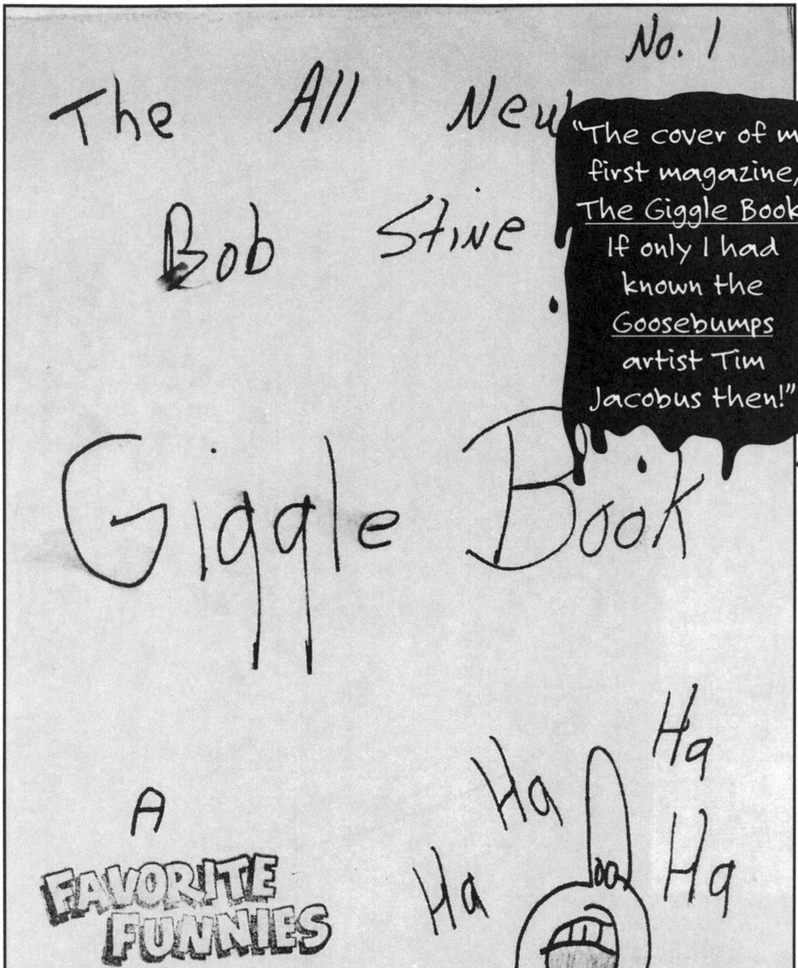

No. 1

The All New

Bob Stine

"The cover of my
first magazine,
The Giggle Book.
If only I had
known the
Goosebumps
artist Tim
Jacobus then!"

Giggle Book

A

FAVORITE
FUNNIES

Production

Ha
Ha Ha
Ha Ha

"I created Sooper Stooge when I was nine. He was the very first character I ever created."

FAVORITE FUNNIES
FAVORITE FUNNIES
FAVORITE FUNNIES
MEANWHILE - SOOPER STOOGG TOOK HIS CLOCK TO THE REPAIR SHOP!
IN 20 MINUTES-THE PLACE WILL Blow up!
There's a repair shop over their!
Oh No! That's the same repair shop that Sooper stooge left the Bomb in!
Hey! That looks like the clock I Gave sooper!
BAM
That's strange! The phantom was blown to bits in the same place I took my clock!
THE END
A
FAVORITE FUNNIES
PRODUCTION

When I was in junior high I created *From Here to Insanity*. It lasted seven issues. And it was typed on *both* sides of the paper. The second issue spoofed Robin Hood. I called him "Robin Hoodlum." (Alert readers of "Robin Hoodlum" will notice some spelling and punctuation goofs, and maybe some odd uses of CAPITALS, but I decided to show it to you here just the way I wrote it. That's because it isn't any more fun looking up the rules in a grammar book now than it was when I was in school.)

"ROBIN HOODLUM by Bob Stine"

ROBIN: "Ah, Maid Marian what say you to taking a walk with me thru Sherwood Forest? What say you?"

MARIAN: "Not me! The last time we walked together I ended up carrying you home!"

ROBIN: "Well how was I to know I'd step on some cactus!"

MARIAN: "CACTUS in Sherwood Forest?! Baloney!"

LITTLE JOHN: "What sayeth thou to entering the archery contest tomorrow, Robin Hoodlum?"

ROBIN: "Fine. A good idea. Come Maid Marian, I'll practice shooting apples off your head!"

MARIAN: "Oh no you don't! The last time we tried that I had to have eighteen stitches!"

"Howdy Doody was the most popular kids' show of the day. My version was pretty wild stuff for those days."

"I was thirteen or fourteen when I drew this cover. Alert readers will see that my drawing style didn't improve. But how about those reviews?"

ROBIN: "Well, I'd forgotten to chalk my bow! It can't happen twice in a row!"

MARIAN: "I know it won't. I won't be there!"

As you can see, I was a weird kid. I spent so many hours—such a large part of my childhood—alone in my room, typing...typing...typing...*just as I do today!*

Several months before I turned thirteen, I began preparing for my Bar Mitzvah. That's an important ceremony in the Jewish religion. I was in my room practicing all the long Hebrew songs and prayers I would have to sing in temple, when Mom came in. She said she wanted to talk to me. She and Dad wanted to know what I wanted as a Bar Mitzvah gift.

I didn't even have to think about it. "A new typewriter," I told her immediately.

My parents really came through. They bought me an office-type machine. We're talking a heavy-duty typewriter here. It was perfect. I used that typewriter for years.

I know, I know. Most kids want more exciting presents than a typewriter. But I was definitely weird. By this time, I was really hooked on writing.

School friends began pestering me to see the latest issue of my funny magazines. They read them, then passed them around. Then they returned them to me.

I loved watching my friends read my magazines in class. The most fun of all was when a kid laughed out loud and got caught by our teacher.

"Here I am at my Bar Mitzvah party. Believe it or not, that outfit was actually in style then."

For example: the time I was in class with several of my friends. The kid next to me had a copy of *From Here to Insanity*. He was reading an article called HOW TO READ THIS MAGAZINE IN CLASS!

The kid was laughing.

"Young man, you're disturbing the entire class!" said the teacher.

"It's *his* fault!" my friend told her. He pointed at me.

I looked around innocently. *Who is he pointing at?* I wondered.

That's when my friend, trying to get rid of the evidence, stuffed the magazine into my hand.

"You, Bob Stine," the teacher said. "Come here!"

It was an order.

The moment I reached her desk she snatched my magazine. "What is this?" she demanded. She held up the copy of *From Here to Insanity* and began reading.

She looked me up and down. "You think you're pretty funny, don't you?" she asked.

"Well..." I started. Modestly.

"You think *THIS* is funny?" She read aloud from the article HOW TO READ THIS MAGAZINE IN CLASS!: "If the teacher asks what you're reading, say it is a pocket dictionary!"

I laughed. The entire class laughed.

"Bob," said the teacher, "I'm marching you down to the principal's office right this minute!"

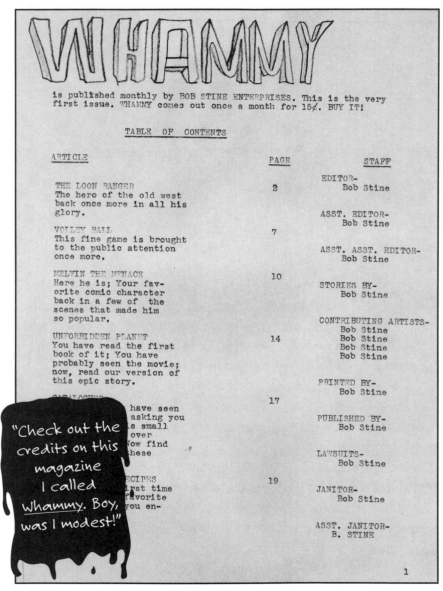

WHAMMY

is published monthly by BOB STINE ENTERPRISES. This is the very first issue. WHAMMY comes out once a month for 15¢. BUY IT!

TABLE OF CONTENTS

"Check out the credits on this magazine I called Whammy. Boy, was I modest!"

1

"When you were a kid, were you called a nerd or a geek?"

o, Bob, what do you want to be when you grow up?" the principal asked me when we were both settled comfortably in his office. I think he was a lot more comfortable than I was.

"A school principal," I told him.

"Very funny, Bob." He sighed. "What am I going to do with you?"

"Graduate me early?"

No such luck. Actually, the principal and my teachers didn't really know what to do with me. I was a good student. I always got A's and B's. But I was never very interested in school. I was a lot more interested in my writing.

At home, my brother and I kept on telling scary

stories at bedtime. One night Bill would terrify me. The next night, one of my twisted tales would frighten Bill out of his wits.

There wasn't any shortage of material. If I wanted to give us both goosebumps, I retold the story of the dead guy under the pile of rocks.

The pile of rocks behind our house.

The rocks were there when we moved in. Our new backyard wasn't nearly as big as the one at our old address. There was a low wooden fence separating our property from the woods in back. In the middle of the woods stood a tall mound of smooth, white rocks.

Who piled the white rocks in the woods? How did they get there? Nobody seemed to know.

But all of us neighborhood kids knew one thing for sure. There was a dead guy underneath.

During the day we used to hang out on the rock pile. But after dark, no one would go near it. So when I told Bill scary stories, I used the rock pile at night as a setting. I made up the dead man's entire life history. Right up until the moment the man was murdered.

In the very room where Bill and I now slept!

Then one day the rocks were gone. So were the trees. A real estate developer cleared the lot and started to build a house.

No one mentioned finding a dead guy. I guess they just hauled him away.

Or buried him under the house....

We never talked about it. Never mentioned the mysterious white stone mound again. But sometimes I think about it when I start to write a new book.

"A nerd or a geek? You decide."

When we ran out of scary stories, Bill and I would go to the movies. We loved scary movies when we were kids. We would go to the movies every Sunday afternoon after Sunday school.

The theater was always filled with kids. We'd usually see a double feature—two movies and some cartoons and shorts. The horror films were always in black and white.

Our favorite films were the ones with big monsters in them. The monsters usually lived in underground caves. An atomic bomb blast would set them free. And they would stomp all over Washington, D.C., and other cities and smash them flat.

When the monsters attacked, my brother and I would scream and kick the seats. All the kids in the theater would go nuts.

Two of my favorite horror films were *It Came from Beneath the Sea* and *Night of the Living Dead*. Do those titles sound a little familiar to you? Sometimes when I'm trying to think up good titles for my books, I remember those scary movies my brother and I loved so much.

A while ago, one of my readers sent a very funny letter. He asked: "When you were a kid, were you called a nerd or a geek?"

Tough question to answer.

I guess I was pretty nerdy. For one thing, I was a member of the high-school marching band, which was pretty uncool in those days.

My instrument was the clarinet. And it gave me a little problem. You see, I couldn't march and play at the same time. Oh, I was a good enough musician. In a chair. But if I marched, I had to concentrate on my feet. Which meant I couldn't think about my music!

So what did I do? I quit the band and joined the chorus. At least the chorus didn't have to march as it sang!

At my school in Bexley, kids hung out in different groups, as at most other schools. There were the popular kids, the smart kids, the athletes, the techies, etc. I never really fit into any of the groups.

I certainly didn't fit in with the jocks. I was a terribly unathletic kid. I admit it—a total klutz. When I was in fourth and fifth grade, we used to play softball a lot. We had a diamond that stretched over my backyard and two others. All the neighborhood kids played.

We must have played a thousand games. And every single time I came to bat, I grounded out to the shortstop. Every single time!

In any sport, I used to dread the time when the two team captains would choose up sides. I was always the last to be chosen. And the two captains would always argue: "You take him!" "No—*you* take him!" "No way. *You* take him!"

I tried playing football. But even though I was always tall, I was a real skinny kid—and I got crushed. I tried playing basketball, and I had no shooting eye at all. I could miss twenty shots in a row—easily.

I suppose my best sport was bowling. But even that was trouble. One day I dropped the ball on my foot and broke my little toe!

When it came to sports, I was mostly good at tuning my TV to the Cleveland Browns playing football. Some people have two left feet. I did sports stuff as if I had three. I couldn't punt, pass, or kick!

But I loved watching the Cleveland Browns (sigh) and Cleveland Indians. Today, I'm a Giants and Jets fan. I never miss football on Sunday afternoon no matter how many books I have to write.

Anyway, I didn't hang out with the athletic kids, or any other group. But I had some really good friends.

In fourth grade, my best friend was a boy named Randy, who lived across the street. Randy and I would spend endless (and I mean *endless*) Saturday afternoons playing Monopoly on the floor of his room. The games would stretch on for hours, and neither of us would ever come close to winning.

One day, Randy's cocker spaniel chewed the *Monopoly* board to pieces. Our games came to an end. And so did the friendship.

In junior high and high school, I had a close friend named Norm. Norm was not shy like me. He was fast-talking and funny. He would go up to strangers on the street and insult them: "Is that really your face, or were you run over by a truck?" Really dumb insults.

"This is my seventh-grade class. Can you
find me? Hint—I'm in the back."

We thought it was a riot.

Norm played the trumpet, a really cool instrument. Norm would make really rude sounds with his trumpet when the band director was talking. We thought that was a riot too.

Norm introduced me to jazz music, which I still

like. He also kept two flying squirrels in a cage in his bedroom. One day, I bet him they couldn't really fly. So he opened the cage door, and they came scampering out. They couldn't fly—but they could leap really well.

We couldn't catch them. They started leaping and gliding all over the room. After chasing them for an hour, we shut them up in the room and went out to ride our bikes. They may still be there.

Norm's father owned the local "art" theater. It was just about the only movie theater in Columbus that showed foreign films. They showed the same Brigitte Bardot film there for at least six years! She was a very sexy French movie star.

You had to be eighteen to be admitted to this movie. But Norm and I, and all of his friends, got to see it in the seventh grade—and every year after that—because Norm always had his birthday party at the theater. And instead of clowns or jugglers, we always watched the movie!

My other best friend in high school was a guy named Jeff. I liked Jeff because he was smart and funny—and because he thought I was smart and funny.

Jeff and I were best friends—and we were competitors. In school, we competed against each other to get the best grades in our class. Jeff almost always won. I liked getting good grades—but I also liked getting laughs. I liked interrupting the class

Top Writers, Artists

The county's best school writers and artists, according to three newspaper judges, are, left to right, back row, Robert Stine and Paul Coleman; middle row, Karen Merc... Halstead and Jeanne Williams and, ... Ronald Steakley.—(Photo

"When I was in high school, the local newspapers had lots of essay contests. I always entered— because I loved seeing my picture in the papers."

ESSAY WINNERS GIVEN AWARDS

Miss Helen Glenn, left, junior vice commander of Capital City Chapter No. 3, Disabled American Veterans, presents prizes to the four winners of the Ohio State Employment Service's essay contest on employing the physically handicapped. Prize money was donated by the chapter and the AFL-CIO. Winners, left to right, are Dave Ballenger, 102 Bishop Dr., Westerville, fourth place, $10 cash; Jerry Mechling, 143 S. Stanwood Rd., third place, $50 savings bond; Bob Stine, 539 N. Columbia Ave., second place, $75 savings bond; Barbara Rall, 696 Vernon Ave., first place, $100 savings bond. Awards were presented Thursday at the Deshler Hilton Hotel. (Dispatch Photo) with a joke or a smart remark. It didn't exactly make me the teachers' favorite.

Jeff dreamed of someday winning a major political office. Step number one was the presidency of our senior class. I was his campaign manager. I came up with his slogan—KICK THE SCOUNDREL IN!

I drew his posters. I wrote his speeches. I even voted for him. Jeff lost in a landslide.

Jeff and I both had tape recorders. The old-fashioned reel-to-reel kind. After school, we'd drag them to each other's houses and make comedy tapes on them. We'd make up characters and act out comedy routines.

We thought we were a hilarious comedy team. We'd usually start laughing so hard at our own jokes that we had to turn off the recorders. I'm so glad none of those tapes are still around today. I'd be so embarrassed!

In high school, Jeff had a little car. The two of us would go to a drive-in for lunch every day. In those days, there were dozens of restaurants where you ate in your car. Young women called carhops took your order, then brought the food out on a tray to your car. When I was a kid, we *never* went inside a restaurant! We always ate in the car.

At our school, you were allowed to drive anywhere you wanted at lunchtime, as long as you got back before the next class period.

Cars were so important to us! The minute we

"Jeff (left) and Norm (right). My best friends in high school."

"This picture was taken at my high-school graduation party. My son Matty tells me this short haircut is back in style now."

turned sixteen, we would run to take the driver's license exam. When I was fifteen, I took driving lessons from a guy who came to my house twice a week.

I'll never forget my first time behind the wheel. I was totally psyched! The instructor showed me how to turn on the ignition. Then he told me to back the car down the driveway. I put the car in reverse, started to back up—and nearly backed over my little sister, who was playing in the driveway!

Bad start.

That's when I got my first lesson about looking in the rearview mirror!

Jeff and I would spend hours driving around aimlessly. We didn't go anywhere, and we didn't do anything. We just loved driving back and forth through town with the radio cranked up, seeing who else was driving around. We would honk the horn and shout to everyone we knew.

Today, Jeff and I don't have much time to drive around honking the horn at people. But we are still friends, and our families recently had a vacation together in Hawaii. His two kids, Molly and Michael, both read *Goosebumps*. I think they're smart and funny....

Those were some of my best friends. Next, I suppose I should tell you about my first girlfriend.

"I really had them laughing!"

exley was a very wealthy community. The Ohio governor's mansion stood two blocks from my house, along with several other enormous mansions.

We lived in a tiny little brick house at the edge of town, three doors down from the railroad tracks. I felt self-conscious because my family didn't have as much money as my friends' families.

My dad worked very hard. He never stopped working! He and my mom wanted to keep us in this nice community. And they made sure we never felt poor or deprived.

But my brother and I still found it hard to fit in to such a rich town. We couldn't afford to drive around in big cars and wear the latest, coolest clothes. Sometimes I felt like a real outsider. For example, in high school, I was crazy about a girl named Lynne. I guess you could say she was my first girlfriend. I liked her so much, my cheeks would turn bright red every time I talked to her in school. I could feel them burning! It really embarrassed me, but there was nothing I could do about it.

Lynne's parents were quite wealthy. They lived in a ranch-style house that seemed to stretch for blocks! On Lynne's sixteenth birthday, they gave her a pink Thunderbird. That was the coolest car you could have when I was in high school.

Imagine how nerdy I felt driving up Lynne's long driveway to pick her up on a Saturday night in my dad's beat-up little Ford.

It probably didn't bother Lynne a bit. But it made me even more shy and uncomfortable. My cheeks start to burn just thinking about it!

I think that my feeling like an outsider as a kid helped to make me a writer. I always seemed to be standing away from the crowd, watching everyone. I became an *observer*, which is part of what a writer does.

Another thing a writer does is try writing a novel. So I did. It wasn't all my doing. In some ways, I have my brother, Bill, to thank for getting me started. You see, by this time my brother was too old to fall for the Grashus Ranger game.

Instead of rebelling against our parents, Bill started rebelling against me. It was very upsetting. One October he actually refused to rake the yard. It looked for a while as if *I* might have to do it.

That's when I started my first serious novel.

Well, it wasn't *serious*. I wanted it to be a funny adult animal story. I called it *Lovable Bear*.

Mom was very supportive of my writing. She wanted what I wanted, and I wanted to be a writer. What I *didn't* want was to work in the yard. That's why, when it came time to paint the garage or shovel snow, someone else had to do it. Someone like Bill.

"I can't rake leaves! I'm working on my novel!" I would cry.

I wrote constantly. I really was obsessed.

I also read a lot when I was in school. I especially liked science fiction. I discovered sci-fi in elementary school. I loved traveling to the future and to other worlds in books by such authors as Isaac Asimov, Ray Bradbury, and Robert Sheckley.

Robert Sheckley wrote a book called *Mindswap*. It was about a company that gave you a vacation from your own body. They switched your mind into the body of an alien on another planet. And they switched the alien into your body. It was a good way to visit another planet. After two weeks, the company switched you back to your own body.

I remembered this story when I started writing *Goosebumps*. I decided to write something with the

BOB STINE

"ELOQUENT INSANITY"

"I kept making my own magazines all through high school."

BOB STIN

"UPROARIOUS UTOPIA"

¡A WORLD OF LAUGHTER!

FROM ONE OF AMERICA'S FOREMOST UNKNOWNS!

"The only difference was, by that time I knew some bigger words...."

45

• R.L STINE •

BOB STINE

presents!

STORIES AND GAGS BY THE AUTHOR OF:

```
WHAMMY
TALES TO DRIVE YOU BATTY
FROM HERE TO INSANITY
HAH! The Maniac's Manual
WOW The Best of Bob Stine
STINE'S LINE Vol's 1 & 2
&  I WAS A TEENAGE SMART ALECK!
```

"...but I still couldn't draw!"

same idea. So I wrote a story about a boy who is unhappy with his life. He goes to a company that will switch his mind into another body. But something goes wrong—a bee flies into the machine. And the boy's brain gets sent into the bee's body! He's trapped inside a bee! The book was called *Why I'm Afraid of Bees*—and the idea started from that book I read when I was ten or twelve.

I couldn't get enough science fiction. That's what brought me back week after week to watch *The Twilight Zone* on TV. Rod Serling's weird, supernatural, half-hour TV show hooked me from the start.

Serling introduced each story. He said we were about to be caught in "the middle ground between light and shadow—between science and superstition." And his voice was so spooky. I liked the whole look and sound of that show. I still watch the reruns today, and I've caught myself recalling certain eerie parts when I outline a new *Fear Street* or *Goosebumps.*

Most sci-fi stories had a wild twist at the end— something the reader didn't expect at all. That was one of my favorite parts of these stories—trying to guess the surprise ending.

I liked surprise endings so much when I was a kid, I remembered them when I started writing scary books. I decided I wanted to have a surprise at the end of every book. Then I decided it would be even *more* fun to have a surprise at the end of every *chapter.*

One of my big opportunities to use my writing

talent came at the end of my senior year in high school. I wrote what I thought was the world's all-time funniest senior-class skit. I called it "TV PROGRAMS THAT HAVE DISTRACTED US AND KEPT US FROM STUDYING WHILE WE WERE IN HIGH SCHOOL."

The Narrator introduced the Announcer who introduced the "Emcee for tonight, a man who is as honest as the day is long—Benedict Arnold!"

Part of the skit was a spoof of an amateur talent show:

NARRATOR: "Another very popular type of television program was the talent-scout program. Talent scouts would bring young talent to the show so that they could perform for the massive audience of TV viewers.

"Sometimes these young talents were very lucky after they appeared on this type of show. Some of them were lucky enough to be able to go back home and get a normal job where they belonged."

The senior skit really had them laughing. *I* had them laughing! Cheering! It was a hit!

Time and again I relived the audience's laughter—laughter *at my words*—all the way to Rubinos, our favorite pizza restaurant! That's where we usually went with our friends on weekends, or took our dates. First we'd go to a game at school, then out afterward for pizza. Sometimes it was a movie and pizza, or a concert

"My official high-
school graduation
picture."

and pizza. That night it was the senior skit and pizza.

Looking back, the one constant in high school was pizza. I've been all over the world. But Columbus, Ohio, still has the best pizza.

High-school graduation was only days away. Life was good.

My mood changed the minute I walked in the house. There was an envelope addressed to me from Ohio State University. Was this a letter telling me I had been accepted at the university? Or had I been rejected? Would the university keep me out because I never took Latin? Because I couldn't jump into a swimming pool? Because I typed with one finger? Because I spent all my time writing little magazines instead of studying?

"In college I became Jovial...."

nearly tore the envelope in two getting to the letter. I shook open the single page and scanned the words.

I was in! The university accepted me!

Ohio State University was only a bus ride away. I could live at home, which was cheap, and keep on eating my mom's cooking, which was delicious.

College life, I learned quickly, is very different from high school. High school traps you in the building all day. You drag yourself from class to class, from morning till late afternoon.

In college, you go to your classes, and the rest of the day is your own. You can do whatever you want. Some students spend it working part-time. Or studying.

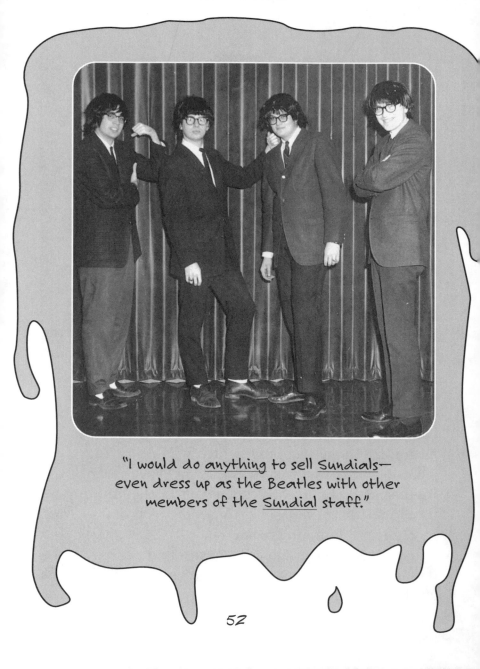

"I would do <u>anything</u> to sell <u>Sundials</u>—
even dress up as the Beatles with other
members of the <u>Sundial</u> staff."

I spent all of my spare time at the *Sundial* magazine office. *Sundial* was the main reason I went to Ohio State. Even in high school, I'd dreamed about writing for that magazine.

James Thurber, writer and cartoonist for the *New Yorker*, was once a *Sundial* writer. Thurber became one of America's great humorists, and I was thrilled to follow in his footsteps.

When he was in college in the 1930s, Milton Caniff contributed his artwork to *Sundial*. Caniff is remembered as the creator of the comic strip "Steve Canyon," an exciting adventure comic that was presented in many newspapers.

For me, joining the *Sundial* staff was a dream come true.

At the end of my freshman year, I applied to the Publications Board to be *Sundial* editor. The board made all of the big decisions about *Sundial*. Professors held most of the seats on the board. They were very cautious people. The chairman asked me a lot of questions.

I showed the board samples of my work. I think they wanted to judge how much of a troublemaker I might be. I tried to look harmless.

It worked. I got the job.

Sundial's sales had not been growing for several years. My goal was to put together a monthly magazine that would give college students a whole lot

'CLOWN' SEEKS STUDENT SENATE POST

Robert Stine says Ohio State students don't expect anything from their Student Senate president and since he's graduating "I'm in a better position than the other candidates to give the students absolutely nothing." Here he hands out literature to a passerby as he stands in front of his campus billboard urging students to "elect a clown" for president. Stine ha~ ~~~~ ~ ~~~ ~~~ of the campus humor ~

"Here I am campaigning for president of the Ohio State Student Council."

of laughs. And the price for all this humor? A mere twenty-five cents!

To do this, we made fun of just about everything on campus. The Deans of Men and Women were favorite targets. It was the Deans' job in those days to punish college students who broke the university's rules.

They sure had a lot of rules. Among them was a curfew for coeds. That's what college girls were called back in those days. This meant on "school nights" the girls had to be in their dorm rooms by 10:30 PM. On Saturdays it was 1:00 AM. Sometimes, for example during homecoming weekend, they could stay out until 2 o'clock! There were no rules for the guys. The guys could stay out all night if they wanted to. Sound unfair? It was.

Sundial made major jokes about this. We pictured the Dean of Women as being totally old fashioned. Which wasn't much of a reach since she was.

We were trying to be funny. But I like to think we did our small part in the early 1960s to bring about change. Soon after, the unfair rules were dropped.

I was editor for three years. I made up the name "Jovial Bob" for myself, because I wanted "Jovial Bob" to be a running character in the magazine. In fact, I liked to think of myself as a running joke.

We printed cartoons, fake interviews, and phony ads in every issue. A lot of our readers were guys. For that reason, *Sundial* featured pictures of a Girl of the Month. First, we picked a good-looking student. Then

"Here is a typical Sundial cover..."

a professional photographer took the pictures. We posed the girl against campus backgrounds such as the famous horseshoe-shaped football stadium.

One month, we decided to play a joke. Instead of running a picture of an actual student, we used a publicity photo of a Hollywood starlet. We made up a name for her—Pamela Winters. (Pamela was my sister's name.) Pamela was drop-dead beautiful.

The interview included this irresistible offer: "If you want to see even more of her—her telephone number is . . ." And we printed the number. But it wasn't really Pamela's number. It was the phone number of the student senate office. OSU's student senate was the college version of a high-school student council.

We had record-breaking sales that day. Eight thousand copies! And all because of the photos of "Pamela Winters." The student senate's phone started ringing. It rang and rang nonstop, day and night.

After a few days of endless calls, the student senators tried to strike back. One of the senators pretended to be Miss Winters. She told the guys who called to "stop by sometime." Then she gave them my home address! Next the senators redirected all of the calls to my home phone number!

My parents were not amused. My sister, Pamela, loved it!

Years later, I used the same idea in a *Goosebumps* called *Calling All Creeps!* The same kind of practical joke backfires—and a boy receives the strangest calls

SUNDIAL GIRL
PAMELA WINTERS

And now *Sundial* invites you to have a beach ball with our Girl of the Month for October, Miss Pamela Winters. Pamela was first hailed ashore right here in Columbus where she makes her home.

"My favorite color is light blue," Pamela asserts. She is very assertive for a freshman in Fine Arts.

"All my friends say I'm assertive," Pamela added. We concurred.

And we're sure you'll concur that Pamela makes a seaworthy Girl of the Month. To see more of her, just turn the page. If you want to see even more of her—you dog you—her telephone number is CY 3-2101.

Ohio Bell will be forever grateful, we're sure.

Photography by Ed Vinton

"...and the famous Miss Sundial,
Pamela Winters."

"I never smoked a pipe, but I thought the pipe made me look like a real writer."

imaginable! I loved practical jokes in those days.

Which is why I ran for student senate president during my senior year in college. The rules said a student had to be a junior to run.

I told the student newspaper: "During the past year, the students of Ohio State have come to expect absolutely *nothing* from the senate. Since I'm graduating this spring and won't be around next year,

I feel I'm in a better position than the other candidates to give the students absolutely nothing."

The slogan on my posters was ELECT A CLOWN FOR PRESIDENT—JOVIAL BOB. We dressed up a couple of *Sundial* staffers in clown costumes and sent them to the campus. Their assignment? Remind students that all of the candidates were clowns—but only Jovial Bob was clown enough to admit it.

Our media campaign consisted of newspaper ads. Ads like this:

As a Public Service
Jovial Bob
Will Not Speak Tonight
in the Delta Gamma (Sorority) House
Enjoy Yourselves!

In spite of an inspired campaign, I didn't win. Out of the record 8,727 votes cast, I got 1,163.

Pretty good—especially since I wasn't on the ballot!

The university refused to put my name on the ballot simply because I wasn't eligible.

What kind of democracy is that?

So how did I get as many votes as I did? Write-ins. My supporters wrote "Jovial Bob" on their ballots.

Which, I think, explains why we lost. Many of my would-be voters didn't have pencils. And some of them couldn't write.

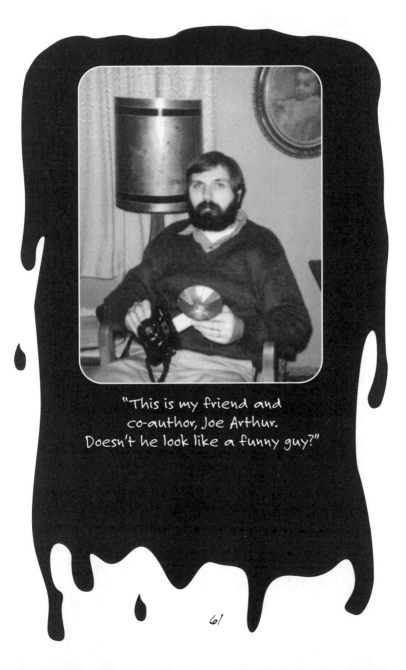

"This is my friend and
co-author, Joe Arthur.
Doesn't he look like a funny guy?"

There were times when the *Lantern*, the student newspaper, suggested that *I* was one of those who couldn't write. The paper made a habit of reviewing the latest issue of *Sundial.* Some of these reviews were downright nasty.

Luckily, other students wrote letters to the newspaper to support me. For example, this nice letter:

> Dear *(Lantern)* Editor:
> I want to take this opportunity to defend *Sundial* and Jovial Bob Stine from the... attack in last Wednesday's letter column.
> The *Sundial* is a constantly improving enterprise, and Jovial Bob is a man of infinite wit and talent...
> I would have made these same statements even if my brother hadn't forced me.
> H. William Stine

I've kept in touch with people I knew in high school, and I have friends from my *Sundial* days. One of them is Joe Arthur. Joe and I are such good friends that I asked him to work on this book with me.

Joe is the funniest guy I know. His specialty is sending the most horrible, tasteless Christmas presents a person can send. Every year, I dread opening Joe's presents because I know they're going to be ridiculous.

When my son, Matt, was born, Joe mailed us a shot

put as a baby present! It was so heavy! It cost nearly a hundred dollars to mail—and the poor mailman could barely lift the thing. I'll say one thing, though—it was the only shot put Matt received!

But here's the *worst* present Joe ever sent Matt. One Christmas, when Matt was eight or nine, Joe sent him *one* walkie-talkie!

Matt was furious. Can you imagine anything more useless than one walkie-talkie? I'm sure Joe will think of something. . . .

When Joe and I were in school, we would call each other after dinner just about every night. We would start laughing about something or other, and laugh till we got off the phone. I have no idea what we were laughing about.

Today, I talk to Joe on the phone about three times a week. We still laugh a lot, and sometimes we still don't know why. I guess that's what friends are for.

I graduated from Ohio State in June 1965.

Suddenly, I faced what they call The Real World.

What I wanted to do was go to New York. That's what I'd dreamed of doing. My bags were already packed. Bill had seen to that. He couldn't wait to get rid of me!

But it takes money. I had a little in the bank. I saved it during college from part of the *Sundial* profits. I just didn't have enough.

Before I could make my New York dream come true, I needed some money. Some cash.

So I decided to rob a bank.

"It was the scariest thing I ever did...."

nly kidding.

Forget about robbing banks. I found a much scarier job. I became a substitute teacher.

I've written a lot of horrifying scenes. But I can't imagine anything more horrifying than facing a new class of students each and every morning.

Everyone knows how kids act up when they have a substitute teacher. It's open season. There's always a kid who claims his name is Pete Moss or Ben Dover or Harry Legg. Some girl who says she's Candy Barr. There are kids who sit in the wrong seat. Kids who don't even come to class.

Scarier than the scariest walk down Fear Street!

After a few months, I was given my own classes. History classes. The toughest part of teaching, I decided, was getting the kids interested in history. Most of them didn't like it. And being an English major, I can't honestly say I cared much for it myself. But there I was. I was a history teacher. I did the best I could.

One of my tricks was this: I told the kids that if they behaved themselves Monday through Thursday without too much complaining, Friday would be Free Reading Day. That meant they could bring in *anything* they wanted to read. Including comic books.

I emphasized the comic books because I loved comic books and I thought maybe some of my students did too. Besides, they might have a few titles I hadn't read.

So we did comics for several weeks. Free Reading Day was fun. I sat with the kids. I read their comics. We passed them around, read aloud. Mine was the only class in the entire building doing such a crazy thing.

It was on one of our Free Reading Days that the principal came in to observe me. The principal was one of those stern, super-strict principals, the kind of principal everyone fears.

I was checking out the latest *Spider Man* when the principal came in.

GULP!

Most of the kids were reading. But not all of them. Several were goofing off in the back of the room. Actually, on Free Reading Days, I had the feeling we were *all* goofing off.

That's because basically we were.

I was on edge, waiting for this no-nonsense principal to say something. He looked at the class, he looked at me. He scowled.

Then he turned and stomped out. He never said anything to me about the class. Not ever. He didn't tell me I was doing a terrible job. But he didn't nominate me for Teacher of the Year, either.

Still, I look back fondly on my one year as a teacher. Even if it was the hardest job I've ever had. I don't know if my students learned anything, but I sure did.

Teaching gave me time to watch kids in action. I was able to listen to what they said and the way they said it. I think my characters' conversations in *Fear Street* and *Goosebumps* are more true to life because of my real-life year in the classroom.

I learned that it's important for a writer to hear how people speak. Sometimes when I start a new book, I picture some of my students and think about the way they acted and felt.

It was a good experience. And I got a chance to catch up on my comic books.

Most nights, when I wasn't dreaming up lessons for my classes, I returned to one of my first loves—

radio. And I worked on *Captain Anything*.

Captain Anything was a two-minute comedy radio program about a superhero who could change himself into anything. Anything animal, vegetable, or mineral. Except his horn-rimmed glasses never transformed.

If Captain Anything became a wolf, he was a wolf in horn-rimmed glasses. If there was some doubt about whether that head of lettuce was Captain Anything or just another head of lettuce, all you had to do was look for the glasses.

My friends and I hoped to sell *Captain Anything* to radio stations across the country. I wrote the scripts. Two popular Columbus radio personalities, Bill Hamilton and Fritz Peerenboom, provided the voices. We worked late into the night at a recording studio in a rough section downtown.

I remember it was kind of spooky because there had been a serious crime committed in the office one floor up. A man had been stabbed right above our studio.

Captain Anything didn't make it out of the building alive, either. We sent records with four sample episodes to radio stations all over the country, but the answer was always the same—nothing doing for Anything.

I did manage to save a little money the year I taught. By June, I figured there was enough in my savings account to pay for a month's rent in New York.

Once I got there, I had to find a place to live and a job. It was sort of like the chicken and the egg thing: I couldn't afford an apartment because I didn't have a job. I couldn't find a job because I had no place to live.

You wouldn't believe the first job I got.

My first apartment was even crazier.

·7·

"I was a writer in New York —sort of...."

icture it: New York's Greenwich Village. Narrow streets lined with brick townhouses and apartment buildings. Crowds of artists, poets, writers. Coffeehouses. Bookstores. Bookstores that stayed open *all night*!

When I arrived in New York in the autumn of 1966, the city had stores that actually sold nothing but postcards. Racks and racks of them. One store offered every imaginable kind of lightbulb. And nothing else! There was a hole-in-the-wall place called The Last Wound-Up. It sold—what else?—windup toys.

And a novelty shop with rubber chickens. We're talking rubber chickens *as far as the eye can see*!

I was in heaven!

But if I wanted to stay in heaven, I had to find an apartment. I picked up a copy of the *Village Voice* and answered several classified ads. I finally put down a deposit on a one-room apartment. It was in the heart of "the Village." On the corner of Waverly Place and Waverly Place. (Really!)

When I say one room, I'm including the kitchen, the dining room, the bedroom, *everything.*

The kitchen had a teeny-tiny sink and a teeny-tiny stove. The refrigerator was different. It was *eentsy-weentsy*! I knew the first time I looked at that kitchen I wasn't going to be fixing any big meals.

No matter. I couldn't afford food anyway. I got the next best thing—bologna.

Every week I bought a loaf of rye bread and one of those packages of sliced bologna. I lived on bologna sandwiches. There were times when my stomach ached from hunger. I even considered leaving my apartment and going back to Ohio.

But I didn't. I reminded myself I had more important things to do. I needed desperately to find a job.

I watched the help-wanted ads. I was looking for work at a magazine. In my daydreams, I could see myself working for one of the big, glossy national magazines that are edited in New York. There was *Life*, *Esquire*, and the *New Yorker*. The only trouble was, those magazines were at the top of the magazine world. I was having trouble getting a grip at the bottom.

My first interview was down near Wall Street. I

took the elevator to the tenth floor of an old building. The office was small. Not small like my apartment. Nothing was *that* small. But it didn't seem big enough for a magazine with the impressive name of *Institutional Investor*.

The publisher, a young man named Gil Kaplan, introduced himself. He asked me if I was familiar with *Institutional Investor*. I'd never seen the magazine, but I wasn't going to admit it.

"Oh yes, I'm familiar with it," I lied.

Kaplan was surprised. And pleased. They had published only two issues so far.

He passed a copy of the magazine across his desk. I leafed through it, glanced at the ads for stockbrokers and investment bankers. What I knew about the stock market you could have fit into my kitchen. And have enough space left over for another slice of bologna.

But I could learn.

"You realize that this is a production job you're interviewing for," he said.

A production job? I wanted a writing job. Still, I was confident. I figured I could learn anything *Institutional Investor* wanted me to know, and I could learn it on the job.

I would have to. Kaplan hired me. For $7,000 a year.

Seven thousand dollars!

I was rich! No more bologna on rye. Now I could add lettuce!

The following Monday morning I reported for work at *Institutional Investor*.

The art director sat me down in front of a table and asked me to put "running feet" on pages. I didn't know what running feet were. Did the boss want me to draw them? Should they be wearing shoes?

I know what running feet are now—now that I don't need to know. It's the printing at the bottom of a magazine page. It includes the name of the magazine, the date of the issue, and the page number.

"You don't know what I'm talking about, do you?" the art director asked. "You don't know anything about production work."

"I know what a dummy is," I told him. "A dummy is a model of a magazine or newspaper page. We did page dummies at *Sundial*."

"That's one kind of dummy," he said, "but there are others."

He fired me.

Had all those years of daydreaming about New York City been just that—daydreaming?

No, they weren't. I soon found another job. And it was a writing job!

The morning I applied for that job, I thought I'd gotten the wrong address. I checked the number on 95th Street twice before I rang the doorbell. It wasn't an office. It was an apartment.

A middle-aged woman answered my knock. She introduced herself as Nancy. Nancy told me she was the editor of six teenage fan magazines.

But not the big-name ones.

"The best-selling teen fan magazine right now is *16*," she said. "We call ours *15*."

I almost laughed.

"And we've got *Mod Teen,* which competes with *Mod Scene,*" she added. "You've seen *Photoplay*? Well, we've got *Screenplay*."

Was this for real? Hey, it was a job. I handed Nancy my portfolio.

She hardly glanced at it.

"I want you to write an interview with Glen Campbell," Nancy told me. She gestured to a lunchroom with two typewriters. There was a young woman already working at one of them.

I knew Glen Campbell only from TV. He was a popular country star with his own variety show.

I'd never seen the guy in my life. And I didn't know where to reach him. "Do you have Mr. Campbell's phone number?" I asked.

Nancy looked at me. "I didn't say *do* an interview," she said. "I said write an interview." She handed me some newspaper clippings and a couple 8 x 10 photos of the singer. Then, patiently, she explained how it worked: "Use these newspaper stories for information. Come up with a story that goes with the photos."

"You mean *make it up?*"

"You got it."

I sat down at the second typewriter. In less than an hour I'd written, "Glen Campbell: Two Men I Call 'Friend.'" It was pure fiction. The article was accepted and appeared in an issue of Nancy's magazine *Country & Western Music*.

I went on to "interview" all of the big stars of the 60's—the Beatles, Tom Jones, the Rolling Stones, the Jacksons. Except I never interviewed anyone. *I made up all of my stories.*

I asked Nancy if the stars we made up stories about ever sued the magazine.

"No," was her reply, "they want all the publicity they can get. They don't care what you write about them—as long as you keep writing about them."

It was while I did my part to help celebrities get a make-believe life that I wrote my first horror fiction. Nancy's boss agreed to try a horror magazine, *Adventures in Horror*. "Bony Fingers from the Grave" was written under the name of Robert Lawrence— my first and middle names. "Trapped in the Vampire's Web of Icy Death" and "It Takes Two for Terror" were mine too.

I worked at this job for about a month. I must have written a hundred phony interviews! Then the company went out of business. I was out of work again.

The fan magazines paid me one hundred dollars a week. My checks were big enough for an occasional restaurant meal. With dessert. And I could afford to treat myself to those great pretzels they sell at food carts on the streets of New York.

But if I didn't find work pretty quick, that's where I'd find myself—homeless on the streets of New York.

And that's when I found one of the weirdest jobs of my life....

"There's a world of communication in bottle caps...."

found a job at a magazine called *Soft Drink Industry*.

My job was to write article after article about soft drinks, soda cans, syrups, and the people who made them.

Sound boring to you? It sounded boring to me too. But at least it was a magazine job!

I wrote such articles as: "SQUIRT CO. NOW USING FULL-COLOR BILLBOARDS." Pretty exciting, huh?

My all-time favorite was "NEW AMERICAN FLANGE HOPPER SPEEDS FEEDING OF RIP CAP CLOSURES." I'm sorry we don't have space to print it here. I know you would have enjoyed it.

I don't want to give the impression that during this time in my life all I was doing was looking for jobs and losing them. I was also looking for girlfriends and losing them.

Until I met Jane.

I almost didn't meet her. It's a long story... (which is why there's no room for my Flange Hopper piece).

I met Jane—she was called Jane Waldhorn then—at a party in Brooklyn that I almost didn't go to. I almost didn't go because it was raining out, and I never like to go out in the rain. And I didn't really enjoy big parties. Too shy.

But my friend Chuck and I took the subway to Brooklyn and found my friend's apartment. The party was big and noisy. Chuck and I hung out together. Then two young women came over to say hello.

One of them was Jane's friend Laurie. The other one was Jane. She had long red hair, beautiful blue-gray eyes—and the worst cold a human ever had.

Her nose was bright red. Her eyes were running. And she kept excusing herself every minute to go blow her nose.

Love at first sight? Not quite.

But two weeks later, Jane's cold cleared up and we decided to get married.

I'm so glad I decided to go out in the rain that night. I cannot imagine what my life would have been like without Jane. For one thing, she is the smartest person I know. How smart? Well, we've been married

"June 22, 1969—our wedding picture.
Jane's the one in the dress."

for twenty-seven years—and in all that time, I've never won a bet!

That rainy night was the luckiest night of my life. And I would say all these nice things even if Jane *wasn't* the editor of this book!

It was wonderful to be young and on the town in New York. It would be even more wonderful, Jane and I thought, if we could find jobs we liked.

Jane was just out of college. She was starting to look for work. I had a job. But writing about root beer wasn't exactly what I'd dreamed of doing.

"Here I am hard at work at Soft Drink Industry with my co-worker Sarah Shankman, who is now a well-known mystery writer."

Even when the editor of *Soft Drink Industry* took me into his office to tell me, "Bob, there's a world of communication in bottle caps!" He was so excited. He held out a bottle cap so I could see the advertising message written inside the cap.

I'm sure the editor noticed that I wasn't exactly jumping up and down.

What he didn't notice, however, was that I used my spare moments to read the want ads.

Just as many good things were happening in my life at this time, there were also big changes in the rest of the Stine family. My brother, Bill, met Megan, his wife-to-be. They were both students at Ohio State. And they both worked on *Sundial*. Bill was editor. He planned to become a writer too. They stayed in Columbus for several months, lived in San Francisco awhile, then moved to New York.

My dad retired, and he and Mom moved out to northern California. My sister, Pam, moved with them. After college, she married, and she and her husband, Kelvin, still live on the West Coast.

Everyone was doing fine. That pleased me. But in the back of my mind, I knew it meant that my childhood home was gone. I was truly on my own in New York.

Reading the want ads finally paid off. One day on my lunch hour, I found another job.

All that remained was to tell the boss at *Soft Drink*.

"You'd actually give all this up?" he asked in a tone that told me he just couldn't believe it.

• R.L STINE •

"My brother, Bill, and his wife, Megan, live in Atlanta now but we try to see them as often as we can."

"It's tough," I told him. "I've liked soda since I was a kid."

"You can always change your mind."

"No, it's time to move on." I sighed. "But I am going to miss the free soda machine here in the office."

The new job was at Scholastic Inc. I was hired as a staff writer for *Junior Scholastic* magazine.

Little did I know when I sat down in my tiny office in December of 1968, that my life was about to change completely.

"I was having the time of my life...."

I spent the next sixteen years at Scholastic, writing and editing magazines—my life's dream.

I started out writing news and history articles for *Junior Scholastic* magazine. A few years later, I became editor of my own social studies magazine, *Search*.

Meanwhile, Jane had also taken a job at Scholastic. She wrote celebrity interviews for *Scope* magazine. She interviewed such people as John Travolta and Michael Jackson. And she *really* talked with them— she didn't make up her interviews, as I had done.

I loved the fast pace of working on a magazine. My magazines were published every week. That meant that we were always working on four magazines at once.

We'd be (1) planning one issue, (2) writing another issue, (3) editing an issue, and (4) proofreading a finished issue—all at the same time.

Today, people ask me how I can write so many books so quickly. They can't believe that I write two books a month.

I always tell them that books are *slow* compared to magazines!

Magazine writing was the perfect training for me. I learned to write fast—and move on to the next piece. I'm a very lucky writer. I've always been able to write quickly, and it usually comes out the way I want it on the first try.

Kids always ask me what I do about writer's block. I have to confess that I've never had it. I can always sit down and write. When you are writing for magazines, there's no *time* for writer's block!

In the 1970s, Jane became editor of the most popular kids' magazine in the U.S.—*Dynamite* magazine. Filled with interviews, jokes, puzzles, posters, and all kinds of zany features, *Dynamite* was a sensation—selling more than a million-and-a-quarter copies every month.

Soon after, I started a very crazy humor magazine for teenagers called *Bananas*. *Bananas* is hard to describe. It had such articles as: HOW TO TURN YOUR UNCLE INTO A COFFEE TABLE and HOW

TO TELL IF YOU ARE AN ALIEN FROM OUTER SPACE and HOW TO TURN YOUR POEMS INTO DOG FOOD.

The magazine had an advice column written by a dog. And a page each month starring a really ugly fly named Phil Fly, who begged readers not to swat him.

My good friend and art director Bob Feldgus and I had the time of our lives trying to make *Bananas* more and more *bananas* each month! We ran ads for "Light Water" (fifty percent fewer calories) and for ice cream that you wore on your face! And we ran helpful articles, such as: 20 THINGS YOU CAN DO WITH A RUBBER CHICKEN.

It was a happy time for me. All those hundreds of little magazines I had put together in my room when I was in grade school had led to this. My own national humor magazine. My life's dream.

During this time, I had several important firsts that I'm very proud of. I was the first editor in the Scholastic offices not to wear a tie to work every day. And I was the first employee to have a rubber chicken hanging in his office.

When I wasn't having fun writing and editing *Bananas*, I had fun driving the other Scholastic workers crazy. I liked to send out fake "official" information memos that looked exactly like the real office memos that were always coming around. My memos were totally stupid—but there were always people who believed them.

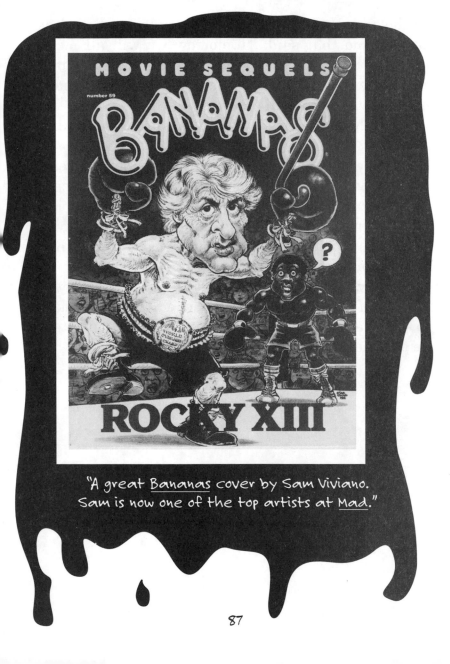

"A great Bananas cover by Sam Viviano.
Sam is now one of the top artists at Mad."

Scholastic had a real office-space problem. So I sent out a memo that said: "Tomorrow we will all move down one office to the right. This will empty out a whole line of offices on the left. And our office space problem will be solved."

Dumb, huh? But a lot of people were complaining about how they didn't want to move.

A few weeks later, I sent around another real-looking notice. It said: "Be sure to wear your raincoats tomorrow and cover up all of your papers. We're going to be testing the overhead sprinkler system all day."

A lot of people believed that one too. I guess they didn't appreciate my "dry" sense of humor.

One day, I was innocently working in my office on an issue of *Bananas* when the phone rang. As I picked up the receiver, I had no idea that this call would start me on a new career.

"My first book and my first bunny ears..."

"My name is Ellen Rudin," the voice on the other end of the line said. "I'm a children's book editor at E.P. Dutton."

A children's book editor? Why would a children's book editor be calling *me*? I wondered.

"I think your magazine is very funny," she continued. "I'll bet you could write funny children's books."

"Huh? Children's books?" I stammered. "I've never thought about it."

"Well, why don't you think about it?" she replied. "If you come up with a good idea, I'd love to publish it."

People always ask me how I got started writing kids' books. That phone call was how I got started.

I spent several weeks thinking up ideas for funny

books. And the book I came up with was called *How to Be Funny*. My very first book was a very silly guidebook.

I wanted it to be a useful book, one that would help even the most serious kid be funny at the dinner table, at parties, at school, in the principal's office.

I was an expert on some of those topics.

The book opened with a test. . . .

Part One: Recognizing a Joke
Here are three items. Only one of them is a joke. Circle the number of the item you believe to be a joke.

1. "Fire! Help! Fire!"
2. "Help! Police! I'm being robbed!"
3. "Boy, am I glad to come in out of the snoo."
   "Snoo? What's snoo?"
   "Nothing. What's snoo with you?"

The book was also filled with tips on how to be funny in school:

The 10-Step Classroom Bumbling Entrance
As a special favor to the author of this book, Harrison Babble, 13, winner of 17 awards for classroom disruption, has agreed to set down for you here all 10 steps to his world-famous Clumsy Classroom Clown Entrance. Here is exactly how he performs it, in his own words:

Credit/Dan Nelken

"My dignified author picture."

"I wait until they're all in their seats. Then, just as the final bell rings, I step up to the doorway and I (1) bang my head on the door frame, which causes me to (2) drop my books. I (3) bend over to pick up my books and (4) all the change falls out of my shirt pocket. Then (5) leaning down to pick up the change, I (6) rip my pants, (7) stumble over my math book, and (8) break my glasses, causing me to (9) walk into the wall and (10) fall headfirst into the wastebasket."

Of course Babble's ten-step entrance (which he hopes to someday turn into a feature-length movie) will go down in history as one of the great clumsy routines of all times. But as wonderful as it is, many of Babble's classmates wish he wouldn't do it every single morning.

How to Be Funny was published in 1978.

At that time, Jane's sister, Amy, was working at the Doubleday bookstore on Fifth Avenue. She arranged for a book signing.

It was a beautiful day in July. My family was there. My friends. The Doubleday clerk piled up several stacks of books. There were extra pens for all the autographs I'd be asked to sign.

I slipped on my bunny ears and prepared to greet the crowds.

Bunny ears?

Bunny ears. Since I was being advertised as "*Jovial* Bob Stine," I thought I ought to wear something other than the usual author outfit. The usual author outfit is a coat and tie. Why not wear something funny? Earlier we had been joking about a sequel to *How to Be Funny*. My suggestion for a title was *How to Be Bunny*.

That's how I came to wear bunny ears to the book signing.

The adults who came by stared at me. You'd think

"The crowds didn't show up for my first signing. The person on the right laughing at me is none other than my friend Joe Arthur."

Credit/Dan Nelken

they'd never seen a writer wearing bunny ears before. Kids stared at me too. None of them would come over. I don't think they liked the idea of seeing a grown man in a bookstore wearing bunny ears.

It turned into a very long afternoon. Guess how many books I autographed and sold?

One.

I decided that maybe next time I'd leave the bunny ears at home. . . .

At my most recent book signing at a mall in Virginia this year, more than five thousand kids showed up. As I stared at the wonderful crowd, I thought about that first book signing and the one kid who bought a book.

People have good days . . . and they have bad days, I decided.

Next I'm going to tell you about June 7, 1980—and why it was one of the *best* days of my life.

· 11 ·

"The Matt Stine Story"

une 7, 1980, was the day our son, Matty, was born.

I watched the whole birth. Matthew Daniel Stine came out looking a lot like Yoda from the *Star Wars* movies. (He's much better looking now.)

These days, Matt mainly likes to hang out with his friends and play his guitar. But when he was little, the two of us were pals. We explored New York City together. We watched old Laurel & Hardy movies and laughed our heads off. We hung out at the Natural History Museum, staring up at the enormous whale. And we played ball in the park... normal dad/son activities.

People always ask Matt what it's like to have a famous father. Matt is very unimpressed. In fact, for a while, I think he was *embarrassed* by all the attention I get.

One day when Matt was about eight years old, I visited his class to talk about writing and to answer kids' questions. Matt hid in a corner, pressed against the wall, and pretended he didn't know me!

Of course, no one likes to have his dad come to school—for any reason!

Jane and Bob Stine
jovially announce
the birth on June 7, 1980,
of
Matthew Daniel Stine . . .

"The birth announcement we sent out looked normal..."

Matt *has* enjoyed some parts of my career. He likes to go out on book signings with me—especially when people ask him for *his* autograph! And he enjoyed posing for a *Fear Street* cover this year. Yes—that's Matt on the cover of *The Perfect Date.*

He and I have always had fun together. If I have one complaint about him, it's that he has NEVER read one of my books! Not one. Do you *believe* that?

As I say, Matt seems very unimpressed with his old man. When Matt was twelve his uncle Rich asked him: "What do you want to be when you grow up?" And Matt replied: "I don't want a job. I want to hang around the house like Dad!"

A Wild and Crazy Baby!!

"...until you opened it."

A few years after Matt was born, I *did* start hanging around the house. *Bananas* magazine went out of business, and I went home to become a full-time writer of books for kids.

Meanwhile, Jane and her friend Joan Waricha formed their own publishing company, which they called Parachute Press, Inc. Jane went off to the office every morning while I stayed home, the happy homemaker.

Photo courtesy of Megan Stine.

"The proud fathers. My brother, Bill, holds his son, Cody, and I hold Matty. The boys are only a year apart and still good friends."

But I didn't have much time to home-make. I soon found myself swamped with all kinds of writing assignments. And I mean *all kinds*!

Here are a few of the things I wrote during this part of my life:

- eighty bubblegum cards for a funny card series called *Zero Heroes*.
- Two computer magazines for kids—even though I didn't own a computer!
- *Indiana Jones* and *James Bond* "Find-Your-Fate" Books, with twenty-five different endings in each book.
- *G.I. Joe* adventure novels, even though I didn't know a rifle from a golf club!
- Mighty Mouse and Bullwinkle coloring books. Hey—*somebody* has to write the words at the bottom of the coloring-book pages! I received five hundred dollars per coloring book, and I wrote two a day. Not bad!
- Many, many joke books!
- Perhaps my lowest achievement? A series of books I wrote about the *Madballs*—a bunch of rubber balls with faces!

I finally switched to a computer in order to handle all of these writing assignments. I was having a wonderful time, writing everything that came my way, turning out book after book.

Then, one day, I received a phone call that got me out of the apartment—and into TV!

· 12 ·

"I MEANT to do that!"

it Laybourne, the producer of Nickelodeon's *Eureeka's Castle*, called to talk about the show. He and I met and had a nice talk. We hit it off so well, Kit asked me to be head writer.

Eureeka's Castle is a program for preschool kids, with puppets and stories and other features. It's a lot like *Sesame Street*—except that we don't teach kids anything! It's all just for fun.

As head writer, I wrote all of the puppet segments for the program. Luckily, I had a staff of about ten writers to help out.

I had never worked in television before. So this was an exciting new experience. When you write books, you sit alone at your keyboard and write. But TV writing is a group project. The producers, the directors, the writers, the performers—they all sit around a big table and discuss the scripts.

Sometimes we would write a script seven times. We would revise it. Discuss it. Revise it. Discuss it. Finally, we would stop when we thought we had it right. Then the puppeteers would go onstage and say whatever they wanted!

I learned a lot about television and about puppets. Being a puppeteer isn't as easy as it looks.

The temperature inside Magellan, our huge dragon, was so high the puppeteer had a small electric fan strapped to his waist. The costume didn't have eye holes, so the puppeteer also strapped a TV monitor to his waist. This way he could see where he was and what he was doing.

Loaded down with the huge dragon costume and electronics, the puppeteer used one hand to operate Magellan's head and mouth, the other hand to manipulate one of the dragon's hands. A second puppeteer worked Magellan's tail. When Magellan needed to use *both* of his hands, a third puppeteer joined the team to work the other hand. Three people to work one puppet!

The personality of Batly, the klutzy bat character, was based on my son, Matt. When Matt was a little guy, his hobby was falling down. And every time he fell, he jumped up and cried, "I *meant* to do that!"

Batly was the same way. He'd fall down the castle

• R.L STINE •

Photo courtesy of Nickelodeon.

"Working on <u>Eureeka's Castle</u> made me
realize how hard puppeteers work."

102

Photo courtesy of Nickelodeon.

"Here the puppeteer blows into a tube so
the Eureeka puppet can blow a party horn."

103

steps, or fly into a stone wall. And he'd immediately jump up and declare, "I *meant* to do that!"

(Matty has outgrown his klutziness. But the last time I saw Batly, he crashed into a streetlight.)

Or *one* of the Batlys did. Truth is, there was more than one Batly. We had a separate Batly puppet just for crashes. When it was time for Batly to fly into a wall, the puppeteer simply picked up the flying Batly version, and heaved it across the set as hard as he could.

SPLAT!

We received a lot of mail from *Eureeka's Castle* fans. One letter came from a mother who told us how much her nine-year-old daughter enjoyed the program. She never missed it. The mother wrote that the family was going to be in New York. She wondered if it would be all right if they visited the set. We said, "Come on down."

We were in the middle of production the morning they arrived. The puppeteers were rehearsing. They had their puppets on their arms.

The girl came through the studio door first. Her mother and father were right behind. The girl looked over at the set. And then she burst into tears and cried for twenty minutes.

Do you know why?

Because she thought the characters were real. She didn't know they were puppets.

I guess that's a compliment.

Sometimes it took three people to work the huge Magellan puppet on <u>Eureeka's Castle</u>.

Photo courtesy of Nickelodeon.

At the end of the first season, we were paid another compliment. *Eureeka's Castle* won an Ace Award as best children's show. That's cable TV's highest honor.

The writing staff and I wrote one hundred hours of scripts for *Eureeka's Castle*. We also put together four half-hour specials. Once they had all been shown, Nick did what every cable channel and network does—they began reshowing them. And reshowing them. And reshowing them. *Eureeka's Castle* has been on TV ever since.

Since we were all finished with *Eureeka's Castle*, I returned home to my lonely keyboard. After writing for TV, it seemed awfully quiet at home.

I had no idea that the most thrilling, amazing part of my life was just about to begin.

"What's a scary novel....?"

ne afternoon, I had lunch with Jean Feiwel. Jean is my friend and the associate publisher at Scholastic. Near the end of the lunch, she leaned across the table and asked, "Did you ever think of writing a YA horror novel?"

"Huh? A *what?*" I replied.

"A horror novel for teenagers," she repeated.

"Well...I've always *liked* horror," I told her. "But I never thought of writing it."

"Well, why don't you give it a try?" she suggested. "Go home and write a book called *Blind Date.*"

"Sure! No problem!" I declared. "Blind Date. No problem. You've got it."

A young-adult horror novel? I didn't really know

what she was talking about. But I never said no to anyone in those days!

After lunch I headed for the bookstore. There weren't many scary books in the section for young readers. I picked up some books by Lois Duncan, Christopher Pike, and Joan Lowry Nixon, and went home to read them.

"It must be nice to be able to lie around reading," Jane teased me the next morning when she left for her office.

"This is work," I told her, turning the last page in a book. Maybe I ought to give scary books a try, I thought. I liked the books I had read. But I had some different ideas.

I sat down and began an outline. It took me a month to outline the plot for *Blind Date*. And it took me three months to write the novel.

One evening I handed a rough draft of the book to Jane. "Read this," I said. "It's horrible."

"If it's horrible, why do you want me to read it?" she demanded.

I explained what I meant by horrible. *Blind Date* is about a boy who starts getting mysterious phone calls from a girl who claims to be his blind date. Only he finds out she's been dead for three years!

Jane liked the book. But, as always, she had many, many suggestions to improve it. I spent another month revising it.

To my surprise, *Blind Date* was an instant best-seller.

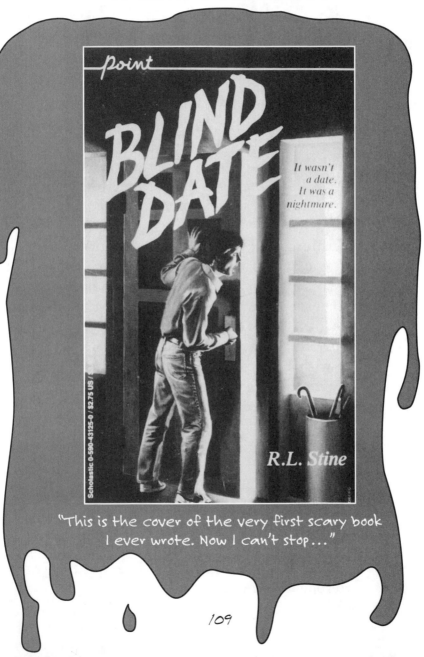

"This is the cover of the very first scary book
I ever wrote. Now I can't stop..."

109

One year later, Scholastic asked me to write a second scary novel. This one I called *Twisted*. It was about a girl who joins a sorority. The sorority has a little secret—every year the girls all commit a murder.

Twisted was followed by *The Baby-sitter*. All three books became best-sellers.

I began to receive mail from my readers, asking for more scary books. I realized that after twenty-three years of writing, I had found something that readers *really liked*.

As I read through all the fan mail, I began to think: Maybe I should try writing a *series* of scary books. I discussed this with Jane and her partner at Parachute Press, Joan Waricha, and they thought it was a great idea. But we needed a name.

For as long as I've written books, I always start the same way—with a title. If I know the title of the story, coming up with the story itself isn't hard for me.

My new series needed a title.

I grabbed a yellow legal pad from my desk. Rolling my chair over to the window, I prepared to sit there for as long as it took to come up with a title.

As I settled back, the words *Fear Street* popped into my head.

I don't know where they came from, how it happened. One moment I was staring out the window. The next moment, I had my title. The words *Fear Street* were repeating in my mind.

Cover courtesy of Archway Paperbacks.

"Matty and his friend Rosha on the cover of a recent Fear Street."

When Jane came home, I ran it past her.

"Fear Street," she said, then with hardly a pause, "where your worst nightmares live."

We had the title!

Series books usually have a continuing cast of characters. I thought I might try something new, something different. Why not have all of the action take place in a single town?

Or a street? An evil street...

Jane and Joan brought *Fear Street* to Pat MacDonald at Pocket Books. She signed up three *Fear Streets* to start. Then three more.

My new career as a scary person was underway. I had no idea just how scary things were going to get.

"I get Goosebumps..."

Fear Street soon became the most popular young adult book series in the U.S. The very first one, *The New Girl*, published in 1989, got the series off to a good start. It was followed by *The Surprise Party* and *The Overnight*, all best-sellers. Soon, I was writing a new *Fear Street* every month.

How did I feel about this?

Surprised!

I truly was amazed by how popular these scary books became. And I was shocked that boys enjoyed them as much as girls. And I have to admit that—over a hundred books later—I'm still a little in shock!

I was working on the first *Fear Street Super Chiller* when Joan Waricha at Parachute Press called me in for a meeting. "Maybe younger kids would like to be scared too," Joan suggested. "Maybe you could write a series of scary books that are also funny. You know. Plenty of thrills and chills, without the gore and the blood."

It sounded like a good idea to me. But once again, I couldn't start without a title.

This time it didn't come easy. I thought about titles for the new series day and night. But nothing came to mind.

Then one morning I was reading the TV listings in *TV Guide*. (I read them every morning. I get a lot of good ideas for titles in them.) An ad caught my eye. The ad said Channel 11 was running a whole week of scary movies. What really held my attention was the headline in bold type. It read:

"It's GOOSEBUMPS Week on Channel 11!"

"Here it is!" I called out to Jane. "Come here! Quick!"

Jane came running to see what the fuss was all about. I shoved the magazine into her hands and pointed to the ad. "The title for the new book series!" I cried. "We'll call it *Channel 11!*"

Just kidding. Of course we called it *Goosebumps*.

I wrote *Welcome to Dead House*, the very first *Goosebumps* book, in a little over ten days.

I wanted *Goosebumps* to have the same kind of feeling you get on a roller-coaster ride. Lots of thrills. Lots of wild twists and turns. And a feeling of being safe the whole time.

"Now I'm scary all the time."

I wanted each book to be as exciting as riding the fastest, scariest roller coaster. I always think of the time I rode *The Beast* at Paramount's King's Island near Cincinnati. *The Beast* is one of the longest, fastest roller coasters in the U.S.

My son, Matt, and I were strapped into the front seat of the first car. Matt was loving every moment of it.

"Put your arms up, Dad!" he screamed.

I screamed too. But for a different reason.

What am I doing up here? I asked myself as we neared the crest of that monstrous first hill. *Stop this thing! I want to get off!*

It didn't stop, of course, and I didn't get off. Yet for a few moments there, as the coaster started down, I thought, *I'm a dead man—this is it!*

It wasn't. What it was, was a safe, unforgettable thrill. The feeling I hope I achieve in every *Goosebumps.*

Goosebumps has become the best-selling book series of all time. It has led to a TV show, home videos, T-shirts, games, puzzles, and more scary products than I could ever imagine!

Kids always ask me how it feels to be famous. I can't really answer that question—because I don't feel any different than I ever did. I think the BIG difference in my life is that I'm working so much harder! Now I'm writing two books a month!

One of the *nicest* things about my success is the wonderful mail I receive. These days, I receive over

"You can't tell from this picture but over
a thousand kids showed up for this
signing—honest."

two thousand letters a week! My mailman *hates* me —but I love reading all the letters from readers, parents, teachers, and librarians.

It's so nice of everyone to take the time to write to me. Sometimes the letters are very funny. Last week, a boy wrote to me and asked: "When you die, can I take over your series?"

One of my favorite letters came from a boy who wrote:

"Dear R.L. Stine, I've read forty of your books—and I think they're really boring!"

"Viewers, beware..."

I work six or seven days a week, plotting and writing my scary books. I work very hard, but I cannot take all of the credit for the books. I have many wonderful editors who help me with *Fear Street* and *Goosebumps*.

Susan Lurie and Heather Alexander are two of my *Goosebumps* editors. They work very hard to make sure each story is as good as the last. They tell me when a story is too scary. And they tell me when a story isn't scary enough. And they tell me when a story isn't a story at all!

When I turned in the first draft of *A Night in Terror Tower*, the two kids in the book—Eddie and Sue— spent the entire story running, running, running.

They ran through the tower, ran from the Executioner, ran from present day to the past.

Susan and Heather both saw problems. They thought maybe Eddie and Sue should slow down to catch their breath once in a while. They thought all that running was boring. I did a *lot* of rewriting on that book—and now the kids run for only *half* the book! A big improvement.

The Girl Who Cried Monster takes place in a creepy library with a librarian who is actually a monster. When I wrote the book the first time, the monster librarian ate *children* who came to the library.

Susan and Heather thought that eating children was too gross for *Goosebumps*. So I put a jar of turtles and snails on the librarian's desk. When he gets hungry, he reaches into the jar and gobbles up a turtle or snail.

I actually think that's even more gross than eating children. For one thing, snails and turtles make a much better *crunching* sound when you chew them!

I *hate* to revise. I think all writers do. I'm always eager to get on to the next story. I hate to go back and fix up the old one. But I'm lucky to have so many talented editors at Parachute Press, Scholastic, and Pocket Books. They force me to make each book as good as it can be. (And they warn me when I've used the name Chuck for a character three books in a row!)

While I'm thanking people, I need to thank Bill Schmidt, who paints the *Fear Street* covers, and Tim

Jacobus, who paints the wonderful *Goosebumps* covers each month.

The idea for the *Goosebumps* TV show came from readers' letters. As soon as I started writing *Goosebumps*, I began receiving letters from kids asking to see the stories on TV.

And now it's so exciting for me to see my characters and crazy plots come to life on TV every week. I watch it every week—even the reruns!

Photo courtesy of Fox Broadcasting.

Who's the dummy?
Ron Stefaniuk makes all the creatures and monsters for the Goosebumps TV show. People say this is one of his scariest creations.

The first *Goosebumps* we turned into a TV show was *The Haunted Mask*. This story came from something that happened in real life.

One Halloween, my son, Matt, tried on a green rubber Frankenstein mask. He pulled it down over his head—and then he couldn't get it off!

He tugged and tugged, but the mask wouldn't come off. I suppose I should have helped him remove it—but instead I ran to my desk and started writing notes. I knew it would make a great plot for a story!

In the TV show, a wonderful actress named Kathryn Long played the part of Carly Beth, the girl who puts on the terrifying Haunted Mask. Kathryn is a very serious young actress, and she worked very hard to make each scene real.

In an early scene, two boys are teasing Carly Beth. At lunchtime, they give her a sandwich with a worm in it. Carly Beth doesn't see the worm. She takes a big bite of sandwich, chews it, and swallows it.

When we filmed that scene, we planned to use a rubber worm in the sandwich. But Kathryn said no. "We need a *real* worm," she insisted. "I can't really play the scene right unless we use a real worm."

So we put a real worm in the sandwich. And Carly Beth bit into it, chewed it up, and swallowed it.

Do you think that's disgusting?

Here's the worst part: We had to shoot the scene *twelve times*!

(But that's show biz—right?)

Photo courtesy of Fox Broadcasting

"This picture was taken on the set of
The Haunted Mask. I'm not wearing
the mask—Carly Beth is."

• R.L. STINE •

I used to visit schools and make appearances at bookstores. But these days, it's very hard for me to get away from my keyboard.

From time to time, I do manage to get to a bookstore to meet my readers. And, *wow!*—what a difference from that day in 1978 when one kid showed up!

A while ago, I returned to my hometown of Columbus to do a bookstore signing. The traffic was so snarled that the driver had to let me out two blocks away. At first, I thought that a car accident was blocking the street. But then I realized that all the cars were bringing people to see *me!*

I had caused my first traffic jam!

One recent book signing was scarier than anything I've ever written. It happened at a mall near Washington, D.C.

I was invited to spend two hours at a *Reading Is Fundamental* book fair. The organizers were prepared for seven hundred people. But more than five thousand people jammed the mall to see me!

They had to turn off all the escalators so that no one would get crushed. Security guards and local police officers had to be called in.

I was stunned. What a thrill that so many people wanted to meet me! Unfortunately, there was *no way* I could possibly talk to all five thousand fans in just two hours.

I had to climb up on a bench and shout through a

megaphone: "Thank you for coming! But I cannot meet you all today! Please go home! Please go home!"

I needed a police escort to get in and out of the store. I really thought there might be some kind of riot.

This was *real-life scary.*

Scary and thrilling at the same time.

Most of my book signings aren't that exciting. But there have been some wonderful moments.

Last year, I appeared at a bookstore in Dallas, Texas. A boy of about nine approached shyly. His mother was right behind him. Gently, she pushed him forward.

"Go ahead," the mother said, "ask Mr. Stine to sign your book."

The boy looked up. He had a well-worn copy of *Monster Blood.*

"Are you really R.L. Stine?" the boy asked me.

"I really am," I assured him. "And what's your name?"

He told me. We shook hands and I asked him if he'd like me to sign his book.

He nodded and handed *Monster Blood* to me. I wrote a short message to him and signed my name.

The boy thanked me, took the book, and stared at my signature. As he moved away, he turned to his mother with a big smile on his face, and I heard him say, "I'm the luckiest man on earth!"

Something about the smile on his face and the way

he said those words really moved me. To think that my stories could mean that much to someone!

Well, I had tears in my eyes. I had to turn away and catch my breath.

Moments like those make all the hard work worthwhile.

These days, I have only one wish. I wish I could answer the question that readers ask me most often.

Do you know what that question is?

"Where do you get your ideas?"

es. That is my most-asked question. *Where do you get your ideas?*

I find it a really difficult question to answer. I always want to say: "Where do you get *your* ideas?" Because we all have ideas—right?

These days, I need at least twenty-four book ideas a year. That's a lot. So I find myself thinking about scary stuff all the time.

Luckily, I've always been interested in stories. I've spent most of my life dreaming up ideas for stories and books. Some of my earliest memories are about stories and fairy tales.

One of my earliest memories is of my mother reading *Pinocchio* to me. I was really young—three or four—and she would read a chapter to me every day before my nap. She read the original version—not the Disney *Pinocchio*. And I remember two scenes from the original book.

In one, Pinocchio gets tired of the cricket's constant lectures. So he takes a big wooden mallet—and smashes the cricket against the wall.

Later, Pinocchio falls asleep with his feet on the wood-burning stove—and burns both his feet off! I was a tiny kid, but I still remember these two scary scenes.

I always liked the idea of a wooden puppet coming to life. In the *Goosebumps* series, I wrote three *Night of the Living Dummy* books, about ventriloquist dummies that come to life. I think I partly got the idea for those books from reading *Pinocchio* when I was little.

I could never get enough stories. In elementary school, I read all of the books of fairy tales, Greek myths, Norse legends, and folktales in the library!

The characters in those myths and legends were like superheroes to me. They all had special powers. Many of them could fly. I read entire shelves of these books—then asked the librarian for more.

When she suggested that I read some biographies of real people, I said no thanks. I never liked reading about real people or real events. I only like reading made-up stories. To me, the real world just isn't as interesting or exciting.

"Where do I get my ideas? This is a picture of my dad. Look carefully. Do you see that small sculpture? It's a lawn gnome!"

• R.L STINE •

I loved stories in books—and stories on the radio and TV. I just couldn't get enough stories!

Halloween was my favorite holiday when I was a kid. But I never had the costume I wanted. I always wanted to be a ghost or a mummy—something really scary. But my mom bought a duck suit for me. And every year I'd go out trick-or-treating as a duck.

Other kids thought it was very funny, but I didn't think it was funny at all. I wanted to be scary—not a stupid duck!

When I wrote *The Haunted Mask* for Goosebumps, I remembered my duck costume and how embarrassing I thought I was. And so I gave Carly Beth, the girl in the book, a duck costume too.

One of the very first scary books I ever wrote was called *The Baby-sitter*. I got the idea from when my brother, Bill, and I used to baby-sit for our two little cousins. We were paid two dollars an hour, which we thought was really good money.

But we earned it!

The little boys were wild animals! They were sweet and quiet when their parents were around. But as soon as the parents left, the two boys became monsters. They would wreck the house. Then they would jump on my brother and me and wreck *us*! They loved to wrestle and fight. They refused to go to bed. They would stay up till midnight, beating up my brother and me. Then Bill and I would struggle to get the house back in shape.

Photo courtesy of Whit Waterbury.

"Matty and my nephews, Sam and Dan, give me lots of ideas."

When they returned home, my aunt and uncle would always ask, "How were the boys?" And we would always answer, "Fine. They were great. No problem!" because we didn't want to lose our high-paying baby-sitting job.

Because of those cousins, I've always thought that baby-sitting was a very scary job. I remembered my scary times as a baby-sitter, and I used some of those scares in the four *Baby-sitter* novels that I wrote.

Where do I get my ideas? As you can see, a lot of them started long ago when I was my readers' age....

Telling my life story has made me look back with pride and amazement. I'm proud of what I've accomplished, and I'm totally amazed that any of it happened.

I'm so grateful to my readers. I'm so thrilled that you enjoy my scary stories so much.

Lately, there have been a lot of rumors that I'm going to retire. But the rumors aren't true.

I don't plan to stop writing these books. As long as you keep reading them, I'll keep writing them!

I still have so many stories I want to tell.

But for now, I have only two things left to say:

Thank you all.

And, have a SCARY day!

"Nadine, our cavalier King Charles Spaniel, keeps me company all day while I write. If only I could teach her to type!"

• R.L. STINE'S •
TOP TWENTY MOST-ASKED QUESTIONS

1. HOW MANY BOOKS HAVE YOU WRITTEN IN YOUR LIFE?

About two hundred and fifty. About one hundred scary ones. The rest were joke books, funny books, adventure books, choose-your-own-ending books, etc. I read an article recently about a writer in South America who has written over a thousand books! Sometimes he writes three books a day! My hero!

2. WHAT ARE YOUR FAVORITE BOOKS THAT YOU'VE WRITTEN?

My favorite *Fear Streets* are *Silent Night* and *Silent Night II*. That's because they have my favorite character in them—Reva Dalby. I love writing Reva because she's so rich and mean and nasty to everyone. She's really fun to write! I have two other favorites—*Switched* and *The Face*. I like them because their stories are very different from other *Fear Streets*.

My favorite *Goosebumps* books are: *Night of the Living Dummy*, *Stay Out of the Basement*, and *The Haunted Mask*. I picked all three of my favorites to be on the Goosebumps TV show.

3. WHAT IS YOUR MOST POPULAR BOOK?
Welcome to Dead House. So far, it's sold over two million copies. *Say Cheese and Die!* is second.

4. WHAT INSPIRED THE *MONSTER BLOOD* BOOKS?
My son had a plastic container of green slime. He stuck it to the wall and couldn't get it off. That gave me the idea for the first *Monster Blood* book.

5. WHO IS YOUR FAVORITE AUTHOR?
I have two favorites, both British: P.G. Wodehouse, who wrote the hilarious Jeeves and Wooster novels, and Agatha Christie, who wrote seventy-nine really clever, tricky mysteries.

6. WHY DO YOU START A BOOK WITH THE "GOOD PART" AT THE BEGINNING?
I like to get right into the action. And I like for the reader to know exactly what the book is about—in the very first chapter.

7. WHY DO YOU WRITE BOOKS THAT DON'T END?

I like a surprise at the end of every book, some kind of shock, something to surprise you when you think the book is over.

8. DID ANY OF THE SCARY THINGS YOU WRITE ABOUT HAPPEN TO YOU?

None of them. I've had a very sheltered life. What can happen to you if you stay home writing all day?

9. HAVE YOU EVER BEEN AT THE TERROR TOWER?

Yes. Two winters ago, my family and I visited the Tower of London in England. We toured the torture chamber and the tower chamber where prisoners were shut away. My visit there gave me the idea for *A Night in Terror Tower*. I wrote the book a few weeks after we got back from London.

10. DID YOU EVER HAVE AN ENCOUNTER WITH WORMS?

When I was a kid, I used to cut worms in half and watch the two halves slither off in different directions. I guess the worms are paying me back—because they keep showing up in my books!

11. FAVORITE ACTORS? FAVORITE ACTRESSES?

Jim Carrey, Bill Murray, Bruce Willis, Robin Williams, Madeleine Stowe, Andie MacDowell, Wynona Ryder.

12. HOW DO YOU KNOW SO MUCH ABOUT KIDS? WHAT'S YOUR SECRET?

I work very hard at keeping up with kids—what they wear, how they talk, what they're into. I spend a lot of time with my son and his friends. I have two young nephews, Dan and Sam, who help keep me in touch. I read a lot of the two thousand letters I get every week from kids. I watch MTV. I read a lot of kids' magazines and teen magazines. I think it's very important that the kids in my books be REAL!

13. WHY DON'T YOU HAVE PICTURES IN YOUR BOOKS?

I think it's much scarier to imagine everything in your mind, and much more personal. An artist could never capture what YOU imagine.

14. HOW LONG DOES IT TAKE TO WRITE A BOOK?

Ten days for a FEAR STREET. Eight days for a GOOSEBUMPS. I also spend two to three days outlining each book first.

15. HAVE YOU EVER GOTTEN A STORY IDEA FROM A DREAM?

Never! And what a shame. I would love to wake up one morning with an idea in my head. But my dreams are very boring. And almost never scary.

16. HOW DID YOU COME UP WITH THE IDEA FOR *STAY OUT OF THE BASEMENT*?

It all started with a crazy picture that flashed into my head. I suddenly pictured a father taking off his baseball cap, and leaves were growing on his head instead of hair. Then I started asking myself questions: How did the leaves get there? Who is the father? Is he turning into a plant? Is he ALREADY a plant...?

17. WHAT DOES YOUR APARTMENT LOOK LIKE?

We've lived in the same three-bedroom apartment for twenty-five years. It's pretty small. I share my office with the dog crate. My son's room is a little bigger than a closet. We have a small apartment downstairs in the same building. That's where I have my pinball machine and where Matt keeps all of his guitars and music equipment. Soon we'll be moving—into a very big apartment around the corner. It has eleven rooms—so maybe I won't have to share my office with the dog! The den is big enough for me to get a pool table, which I'm very excited about.

18. WHAT DO YOU DO IN YOUR SPARE TIME WHEN YOU'RE NOT WRITING?

Well, I don't have as much spare time as I used to—especially with a weekly TV series and so many books to write! But when I'm not writing, I like to take my dog, Nadine, for long walks in the park; hang out with my son, Matt, and his friends; watch old black-and-white movies on TV; read; and play pinball. I have my own pinball machine. It's a great one that Matt and I discovered at Walt Disney World, called FUNHOUSE. Whenever Matt and I both have some spare time, we like to fly down to Disney World. My wife, Jane, is SICK of it. Sometimes Matt and I go THREE times a year! We both want to LIVE there!

19. WHAT SCARES YOU?

I don't scare real easy. But a few things have scared me. I'm not really scared of spiders, but the movie *Arachnaphobia* made me scream. I also found *Jurassic Park* really scary. I enjoy Stephen King books, but they seldom really make me jumpy. The scariest book I ever read was *Something Wicked This Way Comes,* by Ray Bradbury. That book really gave *me* goosebumps.

20. WHAT ADVICE DO YOU HAVE FOR YOUNG PEOPLE WHO WANT TO BE WRITERS?

My advice is kind of boring, but I think it's good. It's that you should read, read, read. Don't think about writing things and sending them off to publishers. Publishers really aren't interested in publishing works by kids. The important thing is to read as much as you can by as many DIFFERENT authors as you can. That way, without even realizing it, you build a good vocabulary—and you pick up all different ways of saying things, different styles, different ways to describe the world, to describe people. I don't think anything is as important for someone who wants to be a writer as reading books by many different authors.